An

Owner's Guide
to
Parenting
Teenagers

An

Owner's Guide

to

Parenting
Teenagers

A Step-by-Step, Solution-Focused Approach to
Raising Adolescents Without Losing Your Mind

by
Pat James Baxter, LPC, LMFT
&
Cynthia Dawson Naff, LPC

REAL LIFE PRESS

DEDICATION

ACKNOWLEDGEMENT

We would like to acknowledge the support and assistance of
our colleagues:

Bob Bearer
Bob DeLozier
Gary Drummond
Jay Kilburn
Cullen Mancuso
Penny Painter

CONTENTS

Contents

INTRODUCTION

Congratulations! You have just taken the first step towards getting your family life in order. Recognizing the need for change and deciding to take action will start the process of "getting unstuck" and making changes happen.

When you opened this book, you had already decided to rethink the manner in which you are parenting your adolescent or pre-adolescent children. Our purpose in writing it is to provide you with practical strategies and step-by-step solutions to common problems.

Parenting is a term which emerged in the 1980s. It involves not only a variety of skills, but also the manner in which you view several important issues. Changes in anything so complex in nature as parenting requires forethought, effort, and practice. The results are not sudden, but evolve. They require a little time. Perhaps an anonymous writer said it best.

An Autobiography In Three To Five Short Chapters

1. I walk down the street.
   There is a deep hole in the sidewalk.
   I fall in .
   I am lost.
   It isn't my fault.
   It takes forever to find my way out.

2. I walk down the same street.
   There is a deep hole in the sidewalk.
   I pretend I don't see it.
   I fall in again.
   I can't believe I'm in the same place.
   But it isn't my fault.
   It still takes a long time to get out.

3. I walk down the same street.
   There is a deep hole in the sidewalk.
   I see it is there.
   I still fall in — it's a habit.
   My eyes are open.
   I know where I am.
   It is my fault.
   I get out immediately.

4. I walk down the same street.
   There is a deep hole in the sidewalk.
   I walk around it.

5. I walk down a different street.

Wisely, you chose to focus on your own learning and skill development. When we change how we act or respond, our thinking and our feeling about things will also be different. By doing this you will insure the greatest possible likelihood that you can influence change in other family members. As you change what you are doing, they will change their responses.

Engaged in the practice of therapy with troubled families of adolescent and preadolescent children, your authors have been involved in developing and implementing the philosophies and techniques of parenting prescribed in this book. We believe in them, use them, and teach them on a daily basis. As a result, we have witnessed hundreds of family relationships change from chaotic and hateful to warm and enjoyable.

Most importantly, we see self-defeating values, attitudes and actions change to self-enhancing ones. Both parents and teens make significant gains in self-worth and self-confidence. These are the kinds of changes that endure, and continue to grow throughout a lifetime.

STATEMENT OF PERSONAL RIGHTS

Each member of the human family has the right to be treated
with respect.

The person and the behavior are not the same thing.

Behaviors may be ineffective, destructive, or unacceptable.

Each person, however, is accepted as having worth,
dignity, and uniqueness.

Therefore, each person is honorable.

Each individual has the right to be held accountable, and is
responsible for his or her emotional state, perceptions and
behaviors with their subsequent consequences.

Each person has the right to the feeling of appropriate power,
which results from self-control and from owning responsibility
for choices, behaviors and their results.

We each have the right to be imperfect, to acknowledge our
errors and to grow from them, knowing that our imperfections
make us no less respected and accepted as a person.

We grant these rights to ourselves, to every other member of our
household and to society.

Authors" Note:

This statement serves as the basis for our beliefs as they are
practiced and espoused throughout this work.

Pat J. Baxter & Cynthia D. Naff

CHAPTER 1

—◆—

WHAT HAPPENED?

At this point you may be wondering, "What happened with the kids? When and how did it all get so out of hand?"

Young people are growing up in a different environment than the kids of even twenty years ago. Through modern electronic media and changing social standards, they are exposed earlier in life to much greater violence and to temptations with more serious consequences. Adult role models are more likely to be television characters, whose values, attitudes, and coping skills have little basis in real life.

Peer pressure plays a tremendous role. Kids today must make decisions that are complex, and well beyond their level of maturity.

Twenty years ago, teachers indicated in a survey that their serious classroom problems were gum chewing, tardiness and running in the halls. Today, surveys indicate that serious problems for teachers include gangs, teen violence, assault, drug and alcohol use, and pregnancy. The consequences of current problems are so severe and so frequent that they have lasting impact on the lives of our adolescents at all socio-economic levels.

Recent statistics indicate that one third of all children are living in single parent households. This is a significant change from twenty years ago. If a child is living in a two-parent household, the odds are that both his parents work. As a result, youngsters have far less adult supervision. They also have less opportunity to learn by modeling the behavior of significant responsible adults in their lives.

Even the justice system has intervened in parenting, complicating the discipline of your child. Parents are charged with responsibility for keeping their children in school, and seeing to it that they function in a socially acceptable manner. Yet, parents are not always supported by the same legal system which holds them accountable.

Today, you may not have the same opportunity to be a role model for your children, as your parents were for you. As a working parent, you may find it more difficult to stay in contact with your child's school or with the parents of his associates. Both are important lines of communication.

It is also unlikely that you have as much time as you might like to teach your child the life skills necessary for survival as an adult. This book is designed to quickly provide you with the tools you need to assist your children in becoming responsible, capable young adults.

Recently, while driving hurridly across town, some unfamiliar lights on my car dash turned red. They went out momentarily, and then came back on. I felt uneasy. Were they signaling immediate danger, or could I wait for a more convenient time to deal with my potential problem? Perhaps it was nothing. Maybe it was serious. I lacked the necessary information to make the judgment. I pulled off of the expressway, parked, and took the Car Owner's Guide from my glove compartment. I opened the book and was able to quickly find the information that I needed to decide how best to cope with my car problem.

Parents also often need a quick reference or guide.

Unfortunately, Owner's Guides come with everything but children. When your teenager's behavior triggers a warning light, this book is intended to help you determine methods and strategies for coping with the behavior.

CALL TO ACTION:
TAKING A LOOK AT THE PROBLEM

Take a serious look at the situation in your home. Below is a checklist of behaviors that may be flashing warning signals. If any of these descriptions fit, it is time to take action.

- ◆ Your child's grades have dropped significantly
- ◆ When at home, he stays in his room and resists invitations to join the family
- ◆ He stays away from home without permission
- ◆ He avoids letting you meet his friends
- ◆ He fails to do chores or to deal with other responsibilities
- ◆ He is argumentative, disrespectful and/or has a poor attitude
- ◆ He no longer seems to want to be "a part of the family"
- ◆ Your child's communication is typically negative and/or demanding, particularly when he does not get his way
- ◆ He demands inappropriate power and control; he often tries to tell others what to do
- ◆ He pouts or blames others, when his own actions cause him unpleasant consequences
- ◆ He confuses endowments or rights with privileges
- ◆ He disappears for hours at a time or even overnight
- ◆ He seems to have a poor opinion of himself
- ◆ What your child considers important in his life is destructive

- He claims excessive forgetfulness, or all too frequently responds with "I don't know"
- He is frequently oppositional or contrary
- He demands to do as he pleases, so long as he "pays for it with his own money"
- His money has disappeared, and there is nothing to show for it
- He disregards curfew.

So your child is not doing well at school, skipping, getting detentions, or hanging with other kids of whom you do not approve. His best friend has dropped out of school. Homework is ignored while he spends hours on the phone or playing video games. Is there a problem here?

The answer is an unequivocal YES! Your child will tell you there is not a problem or that the problem is you. He may say his inattention to homework is not affecting his grades, and that he has a right to choose his own friends. Ignore the excuses and arguments and take action.

NOTE: Be careful to choose strategies you can put into effect. If your teen is larger than you, and expresses his anger by punching holes in walls or uses physical force against you and other family members, you need to consider your limitations. (See Chapter 9, page 81)

WHEN IS IT NOT A DO-IT-YOURSELF JOB?

If, however, you find that your child also fits any of the descriptions on the checklist below it is time to consider seeking appropriate professional help:

- ◆ Your child is sexually active
- ◆ You suspect him of drug or alcohol use
- ◆ He seems listless, disoriented or unusually moody
- ◆ He is apathetic, glassy-eyed, and sleeps excessively
- ◆ Changes in your child's eating habits have the potential to create health problems
- ◆ Your child is getting in serious trouble in school or the community
- ◆ He seems to have difficulty focusing and paying attention, and may be restless, agitated and fidgety much of the time
- ◆ He is associating with kids who are involved in illegal activities
- ◆ He has threatened harm to herself or others
- ◆ Your child has possessions that exceed in value the purchasing power of his allowance or job

Even though you may be having difficulty identifying the source of the problem, let us reassure you that there is one if you are seeing any of the behaviors on this list. Getting professional help is the best way to identify the conflict.

Sometimes it is hard to admit you need help, but finding the solution now is a lot easier than waiting until the problem is out of hand. While it is the most important task we take on as adults, parenting is the task for which we receive the least training and preparation. You do not have to feel embarrassed to admit you need help. All parents sometimes have doubts about their decisions. Even the best of parents may find themselves at the end of their rope.

Where To Look For Professional Help

If you are not sure where to turn , we recommend consulting the following resources for a referral to a qualified professional:

♦ Your child's school counselor or principal will frequently know of a good family counselor
♦ Your family physician or church pastor
♦ A youth services agency
♦ The Department of Human Services
♦ Check the yellow pages for "Counselors, marriage and family, adolescent or child", etc.

It is important to pick a professional who is experienced with adolescents and with families. Look for credentials such as LPC (Licensed Professional Counselor) or LMFT (Licensed Marriage and Family Therapist or Licensed Psychologist). They are an indication of licensure to practice in your state. Do not hesitate to ask professionals how much of their practice is spent in treating adolescents. To get positive results, family and adolescent therapy take special skills and extensive experience.

If you should find effective professional assistance unavailable or unaffordable, work closely with the school counseling staff, or other mental health agencies.

CHAPTER 2

SO NOW WHAT?

By now you may have concluded that at least some of the items in the previous chapter's checklists apply to your child. Is it time to panic or to throw up your hands in despair and ship the child off to military school? Absolutely not!

THE PLAN: HOW TO USE THIS BOOK

Your youngster will not outgrow the problem nor will it disappear. Perhaps you believe you have tried everything. Or, at least it may seem that way by now, but chances are you may have been too close to the situation to see the best course. This book will provide an objective plan and stimulate new ways of thinking.

Many families have learned to behave more constructively and to relate less painfully with the solutions we shall propose. Family members who choose to participate in this growth process learn to live a healthy lifestyle.

Your authors have applied and refined these techniques over years of collective experience in therapy with families of adolescents. We use these techniques daily as we help families learn to think and behave differently. They work because the families make changes together and practice what they learn in the real world.

This book has sections, each of which will give you a part of the plan you need and will also serve as a reference guide. Everything you try may not work, or at least not with your first attempt. Keep in mind that your youngster is probably not going to be happy with changes you are making. He, after all, is comfortable with the existing situation. He is going to resist any changes you try to make, at least initially. Hang in there and keep trying. When your child begins to understand that you are not going to give up, he will get serious about changing.

There will be times when you have to go "back to the drawing board." That's okay. You can revise the plan or try something different. It does not have to be perfect the first time. In fact, to ask perfection of yourself or your child is unrealistic and self-defeating.

An Overview

Section I, which you are reading, contains basic information on behavior, learning, and basic parenting skills, including communication.

Section II covers skills and strategies you will need to effect change and get your family life back on the right track, including the Family Agreement, solutions to special problems, and writing assignments.

Section III explores possible reasons why you may not be getting the results you want, and what you can do about it. These two chapters are devoted to some issues which may be unseen but are highly destructive.

Appendixes

Finally, there are two appendixes. The first contains forms and charts needed for the family agreement. You may copy these for your personal use.

The second appendix is a collections of specific, frequently encountered behavior problems and our recommendations for solutions. Like the rest of this book, these solutions have been used with families and have proven effective.

CHAPTER 3

GETTING STARTED THE RIGHT WAY

In this chapter we will look at key concepts on which you, as a parent, will need to focus. Each concept is an important tool in your plan to create a healthier family.

CHANGE WHAT YOU DO

Remember the little number puzzles you got as a kid? There were sixteen spaces but only fifteen squares. The object was to put the squares in numerical order. But, in order to do so, you had to slide all of the squares around. Because there was only one empty space, moving any square required that another square also be shifted. Changing your teen's behavior works on the same principle. If your child is going to change, you must change something first. What your child is doing works for him. He will not change, until there is movement somewhere else that forces him to shift. That is why you must start by changing what you do first.

Using the behavioral checklists in the last chapter, you have already identified some behaviors you would like to see changed in your family. Now it is time to make a more complete list, and include some examples of those behaviors.

Once you have completed the list, rearrange the items in order of priority, starting with the most intolerable behaviors. You cannot expect everything to change at once. You would overwhelm your child, other family members, and yourself as well. The result would be extreme confusion.

What must change immediately? Start by picking the two or three behaviors that seem most critical. How do you know on what to focus first? Is there a behavior that is dangerous or potentially dangerous to the child or to others? If not, what are the behaviors that motivated you to pick up this book and read it?

In our experience working with families, we find parents come to us with the two primary, critical concerns. The first one is fear based; they are concerned for their child's well-being, or for the well-being of others. The second concern is chaotic family living resulting in misery. Fear and misery are the results of specific behaviors. When we target those behaviors and change them, the outcome will be different.

Living with the status quo is less stressful than making changes. So long as we can tolerate the consequences of our current situation, we will continue to stay on "automatic pilot" and to simply hope for a different result. It is much like living in the desert and having a leaky roof. There is little motivation to fix the problem. There is rarely any discomfort. It is only when fear or misery become too great that we begin to accept the need to make modifications.

This is precisely why your child is going to continue to talk on the phone, until you are sure this overused device will require surgical removal from his head. He will continue to skip school or act as if he has never heard the word "chores" until you do something differently. What he is doing now works for him. He is not miserable; you are. He is not aware of the danger; you are. He has no reason to change.

Where should you start? You are going to help him find reason to change. The next time your child fails to take his headphones off when you talk to him or his eyes stay glued to the video game on the screen, use action, not words. Walk over and remove the headphones from his possession, or turn off the video equipment.

Instead of telling him repeatedly to get off the phone, take it out of his hands and lock it up. Instead of telling him to clean up his room, remove everything left laying where it should not be, dump it all in a box or trash bag and lock it up. When you take action you begin to change your child's comfort level.

Your child will get the message and you will get his attention when his routine is disrupted. Nothing applies here more than the old adage, "actions speak louder than words." When you take action, you send a new message that is far more powerful than words.

WHO HAS THE PROBLEM?

Once you have your youngster's attention it is important to reduce his comfort level. We are not recommending torture, but, as stated earlier, it is human nature to resist change unless we become adequately uncomfortable. Until now you have been the one with a problem. His behavior will not change until you make the problem his problem. Problem equals discomfort; discomfort leads to new behavior.

Have you ever asked your child to take out the trash or to do some other chore, and his only response was "okay, in just a minute"? He continued to talk on the phone or kept his eyes glued to the tube? The chore in question was not done, was it? Did you think you might be talking to a wall?

The usual sequence of events goes something like this. You talked about the issue. Then you explained. You followed with a lecture, then with a threat. Finally, you lost your cool. Your teen has probably built up a tolerance to all of your words. In fact, when you became emotional, your teen went on a "power high" because he enjoyed the sense of control he got when he succeeded in getting you to lose it.

His comfort level was only briefly interrupted. You only momentarily held his attention. Then, you rewarded his inappropriate feelings of power and control. Was this what you wanted to achieve? Your original goal was for your child to be responsible and complete his chores.

If it was not what you wanted to achieve, then it is time to do things differently. Once you have identified what you want to be different, shift from words to actions....and keep your cool. Your goal is to get your youngster's attention and make the problem his problem. Then, he will begin to see the need for change.

REWARDS AND OTHER CONSEQUENCES

Using rewards and consequences requires thought. It is important to know what you want to accomplish when you reward or give consequences to your child.

Anyone who has ever gone to the grocery store more than a couple of times has seen "the scene": A small child is sitting in the grocery cart pushed by a tired parent who just wants to get the weekly shopping finished. Child spies something he wants and starts whining. Mom says, "No, wait till we get home and you can have something then." The drama begins. The child begins to whimper and then to cry and finally works himself into a howling, ring-tailed fit. By this point Mom is worn out and looking embarrassed. How does she solve the dilemma? She gives this little tempest a cookie, if he promises to be quiet.

What does the tot learn from this experience? That he should not throw temper tantrums when he is unhappy? Was that not Mom's intent...... to stop the tantrum throwing behavior? That may have been Mom's intent but it is definitely not what the child learned. He learned that throwing a temper tantrum in the grocery store gets him a cookie. If you are a betting person, you will know on whom to put your money come next shopping trip. The little rascal now knows exactly how to get himself a cookie in the grocery store.

If you are assuming this only happens with toddlers, we have news! We recently encountered a thirteen year old youngster who persisted in causing trouble at school. Mom promised Jenny $25 if she would behave. Jenny began to terrorize the staff of the school after-care program where she was enrolled. The staff was ready to evict her from the program. Mother promised again to pay her, if only she would behave. Needless to say, the fits have continued. The next time it was in the Doctor's office.

Why should it stop? It was a profitable venture for Jenny. We have encountered many similar situations where parents have made a practice of offering bribes to stop unwanted behaviors. Instead, the bribe only encouraged and strengthened the problem behavior. Be careful to reward only the long term behavior that you want.

Sometimes it is not apparent that we are rewarding the child for his behavior. Dan, a preteen in our treatment program threw a full blown temper tantrum that required he be restrained and given a time-out. Because he had not eaten, Dan's parents brought him a hamburger and fries. Dan seemed pleased to have his favorite fast food. What did his parents actually accomplish? They sent the message that it was still business as usual despite an exhausting episode of inappropriate behavior.

Dan's parents were puzzled by this at first. They did not stop to think that a hamburger and fries were anything more than something to satisfy hunger. When they learned to see the situation through their son's eyes, they realized they had rewarded his behavior. Better they had brought him a meal that was nourishing, but less a child's favorite.

A local elementary school principal does not allow children at her school to serve out suspension at home. They spend their suspension doing school work while sitting in her office. She has learned they would like nothing better than to go home, where they do not have to work or pay attention in class. She avoids rewarding inappropriate class room behavior by keeping them in her office doing written school work.

Whenever undesirable behavior persists, it is time to reconsider what the youngster might be getting out of his situation. Try to look at it from his point of view. We shall deal with rewards and consequences at greater depth in Chapter 6.

Why Has The Behavior Not Stopped?

Any behavior that has continued must in some way have been reinforced! Either inadvertent responses on the part of others or failure to take action has reinforced the behavior. Look for ways that your child may be getting rewarded, ways that may not be obvious to you at first glance.

YOUR REACTION MAY BE A REWARD

Your reaction alone can serve as a reward or reinforcement. Yelling, lecturing and getting angry are clues you may be overreacting. If you let your child "push your buttons" you may be reinforcing the very behavior you are attempting to eliminate. He may be getting a "rush" out of seeing you fly off the handle.

By overreacting in this fashion, we not only reward "button pushing" behavior, but model coping with difficulty by losing self-control. Refusing to lose your composure sends a clear message that you have the strength to protect your child from himself and from the world.

Learn to react to situations calmly, by simply acknowledging the behavior and giving your child an appropriate consequence with little or no explanation.

You shall have acknowledged and not ignored the problem. You stayed in control, and by giving consequences you made it clear that the behavior was not going to be tolerated.

WHEN TO REWARD

You are absolutely correct if you think that certain levels of behavior should be expected without a reward. You should not have to reward someone for behaving like a human being!

Make it clear that you expect consideration, courtesy and good manners. If you begin rewarding minimal and basic human behaviors, your youngster may become resistant to doing anything without reward.

ACKNOWLEDGEMENT IS A KEY

Sometimes kids really want nothing more than to have their actions or efforts acknowledged. When your child makes an effort to change, or tries a new skill, it is important to encourage even imperfect effort. You can expect that there will be setbacks along with the successes.

The following points should be kept in mind:

- Start by acknowledging the change or accomplishment. Sometimes, all your child really wants is assurance that you have noticed his effort: "I see that you mowed the lawn."
- Given the opportunity, your child may be his own best critic. Rather than finding fault with his job, ask him, "How do you feel about the job you did?", "your behavior now?", or "how you handled that?" He will probably come up with his own ideas for improvement.
- What do you do if he does not see anything wrong with his accomplishment or behavior? Try this, " I see you are really trying. How do you think you might do even better next time?"

Often after a youngster has accomplished a task or improved a behavior, it is important to ask him, "How do you feel about yourself now"?

By asking this question and acknowledging his response you can help reinforce the changed behavior and let him know that he is important. You will also help him become aware of differences in his feelings about himself. The time you take to notice your child's changing behavior is the most important reinforcer you have.

Rewarding your child appropriately requires forethought. Be aware of what you want to accomplish when you give rewards and consequences.

(Note: Some kids will purposely try to avoid doing their best. If you suspect this to be the case, pay special attention to the chapter on Power & Control).

STAND UNITED

Children learn to sense tension or disagreement between parents at a very early age, and may respond to it in a variety of ways. Parental tension initially results in anxiety or uncertainty for the child, who senses instability in the family. From early on, they may learn to engage in attention-getting devices as they solicit reassurance from the parent that everything will be okay.

Negative attention-getting devices defocus parents from their own personal or marital relationship issues. As the parents unite to focus on the child's misbehavior, the original tension and anxiety begin to subside in all three players, if only briefly.

Reducing anxiety is highly reinforcing. Therefore, the child is very likely to repeat the attention-getting response the next time he senses tension in the parental relationship and/or feels anxious. Keeping attention focused on himself also increases his sense of security.

Likewise, it is tempting for the parent to continue to react to the distraction. He also wants relief from his tension which has been provoked by marital or personal conflict.

On the other hand, an older child may use conflict between parents to "divide and conquer" them in order to get his way about something. This strategy works especially well for youngsters, unless parents are prepared to hang in there together and communicate.

If both parents work or there is a divorce, it may be difficult to communicate as adequately as would be ideal. Even savvy parents, who pride themselves on doing the parenting thing together, occasionally get duped by their kids.

Has your child ever elicited a "yes" from you, only to learn that your spouse had just told him "no"? If you have been on either side of this parenting dilemma, you know what it is like to be manipulated. Many situations really do not require an immediate decision. "Let me think about it," is often quite adequate for the present. Then get back with him after thinking about it or checking things out. Ambiguous final responses are unfair, and invite problems.

Most parents occasionally disagree about parenting issues. Try to anticipate differences you and your spouse may have about parenting and come to agreement before the issue surfaces.

When an unanticipated issue surfaces simply back your spouse on the issue until you can discuss it in private. Always make a point of resolving your disagreements out of your child's earshot. There is no harm in occasionally deciding as a parenting team to do something different. Simply tell your child that Mom and Dad have changed their mind about the situation.

If your children are manipulating you and your spouse, or telling different versions of the same story to the two of you, be on the alert. Check with other authority figures in your child's life, his teachers, baby-sitters, daycare, etc., to be sure you are hearing everything you should.

Jake, a teenager in our treatment program recently told his mother he would not be required to attend therapy one night because it was only for kids who were graduating from the program. By the time Jake's mother was made aware of the truth, he had disappeared for the evening. Do not hesitate to check out your child's story .

Again, we would like to stress a point we made earlier in this section. If, as parents, you continuously disagree about the rules and consequences for your child, consider other factors. Should you find that you are constantly arguing or fighting with your spouse (or ex-spouse) about child-rearing issues, then perhaps the core issue is in your relationship with one another. We suggest you consult Chapter 11, "At The End of Your Rope".

Kids are ingenious at picking up on the signals that you and your spouse send out. Radar has nothing on them. It is of ultimate importance that parents agree to expect the same standards of behavior and impose the same consequences. They must communicate clearly with each other. If you disagree about any element of your child's upbringing, it is important to work it out in private. Stand united.

KNOW WHAT IS EXPECTED

As we said earlier, no one gets any preparation or training to be a parent. Yet your approach does not have to be by trial and error. You can sway the odds by developing a clear mental picture of your role and that of your child. Parent and Kid Roles are listed in Appendix I.

"If at first you don't succeed, try, try again." It's old and worn, but still true. Many parents give up too quickly when they try a new angle and the desired results are not immediately observable.

The world is a scary place for kids; there are a lot of unknowns out there. Children need to feel assured that someone is nearby who can protect them from that world. They have a right to expect it.

The limits you set and the consistency with which you enforce those limits, are a primary means by which children confirm your strength and reliability. They often persist in unacceptable behavior because of a need to test your ability to stand firmly behind what you say that you will do. Predictability equals security.

Some kids need only test a couple of times before they believe you are going to stick to your guns. But others need to test, test, and retest. When out of frustration and exhaustion you give in to your child's demands, you have increased his tolerance for lengthy argument. He will also continue to test the limits.

He gets two messages when this happens. One message is "If I keep it up, eventually Mom and Dad will let me have my way." This reinforces his desire for inappropriate power and for immediate gratification. The second message is both more subtle and more harmful: "If they gave in, then I am stronger than they are.

I do not believe that I can cope with everything in that world out there, yet they are weaker than I. Therefore, I cannot be secure of survival." The child's insecurity and his frequent retesting are likely outcomes, when parents fail to stand up reasonably well to their kid's excessive or unhealthy demands.

For your child to develop healthy behavior patterns, your persistency and consistency are necessary. Learn to outlast your child. He needs to be able to expect that you will not let him have too much freedom in a world he finds scary.

PARENTS AND FRIENDS

Ever remember saying as a teen, "I'm never going to treat my kids the way my parents treat me"? You are not alone. Most of us said it at one time or another. Lots of people have reacted to memories of their teen years by trying to do things quite differently. Occasionally, the result is an adult who tries to be their kid's best friend. Your youngster has peers who are his friends. He needs responsible parents who recognize that it is their job to assume the parent role.

There are also parents who apparently believe that it is not okay for their child to be angry with them. All children are sometimes angry with a parent. Love and anger have nothing to do with each other. Anger is a response to frustration, and frustration tolerence is something we must teach our kids. It's important to recognize that it is okay for us to feel angry. The extent to which we may excelerate the emotion and how we behave in response to the feeling of anger are choices we make.

For any of us, the only feelings over which we have control are our own. If your child accuses you of making him unhappy, remind him that he makes the choice to be unhappy. When we insist on the individual taking responsibility for his own actions and feelings, he eventually learns to "own" them.

In the mean time, you may have to accept the notion that your child may be angry with you occasionally, especially when you begin to make changes. After all, he was comfortable doing what he was doing. He will resent having his apple cart upset. Again, it is important to be your child's parent, not his friend.

In one of our teenage therapy groups, we recently asked the kids how they thought a good parent should act. Most of these kids have had the experience of being parented by an unsure parent, and now enjoy the security that comes with being parented by someone who has become more confident with their skills. We include the following list because so many parents have difficulty accepting the concept that kids really do want and need to have limits set and enforced.

The kids believe a good parent should:

1. Lay down rules.
2. Act like you want us to act.
3. Don't be afraid to confront inappropriate behavior.
4. Give us recognition for trying.
5. Tell us how you feel and show affection.
6. Keep your promises.
7. Listen.
8. Make the decisions.
9. Don't fall for our guilt trips.
10. Insist we respect your boundaries and respect ours.
11. Give us appropriate consequences.
12. Don't give in to us.
13. Give us more than rules.
14. Get involved with our schooling.
15. Spend quality time with us and do things with us.
16. Don't worry about being perfect; just keep trying.
17. Don't tolerate inappropriate behavior.
18. Don't take responsibility for making us happy.
19. Stick together as parents.
20. Give yourself personal time.

Again, kids want limits. They need limits to feel safe and they know that it requires a responsible parent to establish and enforce such limits. Acting like a parent toward your child conveys the message you will keep him safe.

The same group of adolescents believed kids should:

1. Have respect for parents, siblings, friends and all others.
2. Be honest, no lying or stealing.
3. Do your best in school.
4. Respect authority.
5. Do not try to tell your parents or other adults what to do.
6. Stay away from drugs, alcohol and kids who do them.
7. Have a good attitude.
8. Be responsible for your own attitude, feelings and behavior.

How you see your roles as parent and child is going to be a little different in each family, but the basic principles we outlined above should apply. In short, know what you expect of yourself as a parent, what you expect of your child. Know your roles as parent and child.

Now you have a picture of how parenting should look. Here are the four concepts you need to keep in mind:

- ◆ Change what you do: more action, less talk.
- ◆ Use rewards and consequences effectively.
- ◆ Stand United.
- ◆ Parent and child roles are different.

CHAPTER 4

HOW TO SPEAK THE SAME LANGUAGE AS YOUR CHILD

Many parents reach the frustrating conclusion that kids today speak a different language. True, contemporary kids use expressions that are foreign to us. But at their age we used expressions strange to our parents. Communicating effectively with your adolescent is no different than communicating effectively with any other person. The same rules apply.

LEARNING TO LISTEN

Even though you may not agree with what is being said, it is important to assure the speaker, in this case your child, that you are listening. Ignore surrounding distractions and make eye contact as he speaks.

Try not to focus on whether you agree or disagree but instead, concentrate on hearing what your child said. Many parents jump in and "correct" their teen's opinion, request or inquiry without taking the time to acknowledge what they heard. The result is a teen who thinks his parent did not really listen.

Assuring Your Child You Understand

Next, summarize what you heard your child say so that he knows that you understood him. You can summarize using your teen's words or try to put it in your own, being careful the content doesn't change "in the translation." An appropriate summary might start this way: "Let me see if I understand. You are saying that......"

If your teen confirms that you understand, then continue. If not, ask him to restate what he has said and then summarize again.

Use a calm voice and keep the volume appropriate. If you feel unable to avoid yelling, let your teen know the conversation will have to be continued at a later time. Let him know as specifically as possible when that will be.

Sort Out Thought From Feeling

As you summarize, try and determine whether your adolescent expressed a thought or a feeling. If he used feeling words to express thoughts or vise versa, point out the discrepancy. For example "Did you mean you thought (instead of felt) you should be allowed to sleep over at Tracie's tonight?" By the way, pointing out discrepancies in your teen's statements by using questions is more productive than using declarative statements. When you use corrective statements such as "No, you meant that you thought you should get to go to the movies," the person is more likely to become defensive.

USE "I FEEL" STATEMENTS

Being aware of the difference between thoughts and feelings is important for clear thinking. In order to express feelings, use the following format and ask your teen to do the same:

> *"I feel* (emotion you are experiencing at the moment)
> *When* (describe what happened or what was said, in the third person if possible)
> *The message I get is* (describe the real message you are receiving from the action or statement in question).
> *What I would prefer is* (describe what you would like to have happen next time)

The following is an example of how you might use an "I feel" statement appropriately when your teen fails to take out the garbage: "I feel frustrated when the garbage can is allowed to over-flow. The message I get is that you do not believe you should contribute to the care of your own home. What I would prefer is that you take out the garbage when you find the can full."

TAKING RESPONSIBILITY FOR FEELINGS

By using "I feel" statements you will promote more open and honest communication with your youngster. You will also help your teen and yourself take responsibility for feelings.

It is important to remember that no one can make you feel anything you do not choose. When you tell your child he is making you angry or upsetting you, you give him control of your emotions. You also send him the message that he can blame others for how he feels. So long as he believes he can continue to blame others for his feelings he is going to blame them for his actions as well. If you hear statements such as "I couldn't help it", or "He made me do it", then your child is shifting responsibility for his feelings and actions to others. Your child's behavior will not improve much as long as he continues with this kind of thinking. Learn to model responsibility for your own feelings, and teach your teen to do the same.

TIPS TO AVOID ARGUMENTS

If the subject you are discussing with your teen is a heated topic, keep these guidelines in mind:

1. Stick to the present situation. Dragging up the past is rarely productive.
2. Describe situations in the third person. Avoid statements that begin with "you"; they tend to sound blaming.
3. Use "I feel" statements to express emotions.
4. Talk in specifics rather than generalities.
5. Try to avoid "black and white" thinking. Words such as *never, ever* and *always* are likely to indicate extreme thinking. There are most always exceptions. Talking in extremes leads to deflection from the topic under discussion.

It's also important to listen for areas of agreement. Possibly you and your adolescent want the same thing or have the same goal, but you are simply expressing it differently. Be sure to point out where you see areas of agreement.

It may be reasonable and helpful to offer a choice. For example, "No, tonight is a school night. You may not spend the night at Lisa's house. But you can talk to her on the phone for a half hour, or you can invite her to spend Saturday night with you."

HAS YOUR TEEN MADE ARGUING AN ART FORM?

If your teen still persists in arguing, then he is probably engaged in a power struggle with you (for other power and control issues see Chapter 10, Power Battles). You are going to need to use all of the communication tools we just discussed plus the following strategies.

A LAWYER IN THE HOUSE

If you are beginning to think you have a potential lawyer living at your house, then arguing with your child is probably taking up much of your time. Arguing is a difficult habit for your child to break, because it is generally learned over a long period of time. All the kid has to do is say "So?", and he has closed out even the most logical explanation.

An explanation is not really what he wants, even though explaining is where it probably began. When kids are little it is natural for them to ask "why". They really do want to understand their world. But as they get older lots of kids, particularly smart kids, figure out that if they can get you to explain "why" then they can counter with "why not".

We adults often fall easily into the trap of giving explanations, in order to satisfy our own need to defend our decisions. We would really like for our kids to understand and to be pleased with us.

Your child's agenda is different at this point. When you explain to kids who are into arguing, they are going to use the explanations for ammunition to continue the argument. The real agenda is different from the stated agenda. Understanding is not what your child really desires. What he really wants is control.

A statement such as the following may make some difference.

"I'm concerned when I hear you argue like this. I wonder when you will begin to excercise the mature reasoning that is required for the freedoms you want to have."

Lecturing is another trap. It effectively teaches kids how to argue. Lecturing employs a style of rhetoric that closely resembles arguing, and it provides ammunition for argument. Kids learn how to "tune out" lectures, and that alone tends to increase their stamina during arguments. Stop talking. Take action.

IT TAKES TWO TO PLAY

The key then in stopping the arguments is to quit participating. The original answer given is the one to which you are going to adhere, so you must think carefully before making a response you may regret.

You can make your decision clear by refusing to give explanations when your child demands to know "WHY?". The only answer you need to give is a simple one such as "because that is what I have decided". In this way you avoid providing ammunition for argument.

If your teen persists in trying to elicit further information then it is time to let him know there will be consequences. "If you persist in trying to argue with me you will lose your phone privileges (stereo, TV, etc.) for the rest of the day (2 days, etc.)" is an appropriate response to your child at this point. When your teen persists, then interrupt him. Tell him his privilege is gone for the stated period of time and walk away.

For kids and teens who argue chronically, or for those who seem unaware of what they are actually saying, a tape recorder is an important tool. Record the arguments and play them back for your teen after you both have had time to calm down. Point out the relentlessness, the disrespect, the rudeness, the interrupting he does. It is important to be specific, so that he knows exactly what he needs to change.

WHAT ARE YOU MODELING?

It is also important you look at your own style of handling conflicts. Are you and your spouse modeling arguing for your child? Do you interrupt each other? Do you lecture? If you are lecturing or arguing, then STOP!

If your child is good at the game he will probably respond with " well, you do it". Part of his game is to get you focused on something besides his own behavior. When you hear this deflection, remind him "We aren't talking about me right now; we're talking about you. We all have problems. I will work on mine, but you need to work on your own".

In summary, the key to ending the arguments is to stop explaining, stop lecturing, and stop giving in. Model positive conflict resolution.

SECTION II

CHAPTER 5

DEVELOPING THE FAMILY AGREEMENT AND TOKEN SYSTEMS

WHAT IS THE FAMILY AGREEMENT?

The family is a "mini learning laboratory", in which a child must develop the belief systems and skills he will use to function in that big world outside his own front door. It is in our home and family that we learn to become accountable for our actions, and to cope productively with the demands of society.

In order to share in the resources of our country, we are expected by society to assume the responsibility of contributing in a manner proportionate to what we consume. We gain self-worth and a sense of belonging by contributing, rather than consuming.

We have formal written rules in society, which we call laws. Breaking a law results in consequences which limit our freedom and privileges. If we speed, we pay a fine. If we drive recklessly, we may lose the privilege of driving. If we seriously disregard the rights of others, we may lose our freedom through incarceration.

The Family Agreement is a formalized written contract between parents and each child. It clearly communicates the rules or laws of the household, the behavioral expectations for the children, and the freedoms and privileges that may be expected for various levels of maturity and responsibility. By understanding the importance of these rules and expectations, your child develops an understanding of how society's rules work.

"But I don't have time"

More than likely, you don't have time not to! Besides, we have provided you with fill-in-the-blank forms and a Sample Agreement. They are concise, almost self-explanatory, and considerably reduce the amount of time you will spend in preparation and maintenance. You will find copies of the blank forms we use in Appendix I. Feel free to copy them for your personal use.

How do we begin?

It is most important that both parents work together in developing and in maintaining family agreements. You will probably want to devise age appropriate agreements for each child. We have seen it done quite successfully with even pre-school age children. The agreements are easy, effective, and efficient — especially when you get the hang of it. On the next pages are the Family Agreement and a sample of the point chart, both of which are essential to the effectiveness of the concept.

THE FAMILY AGREEMENT 1

(family name)

Compliance with these basic rules allows me to be a member in good standing of my family and society:

- ♦ No physical violence to people or property
- ♦ No verbal abuse (cursing, insults or threats)
- ♦ No defiance of parents, teachers, or any other authority figures
- ♦ No drugs (including alcohol)
- ♦ No skipping classes
- ♦ No absence from home without permission
- ♦ No dishonesty (no lieing, no leaving out important facts)
- ♦ No stealing
- ♦ No association with acquaintances unacceptable to parents
- ♦ _____
- ♦ _____

I accept responsibility for abiding by these Basic Rules and understand that any violation of them results in immediate loss of freedom and privileges for a specifed period of time. Parents may assign additional consequences they believe appropriate.

I agree that my freedom and privileges(page 2 of this agreement) shall be determined by the degree to which I fulfill my obligation as outlined in the Weekly Responsibility Schedule attached to this agreement. I also agree that I will attend the Weekly Family Meeting which is held on _____ (day) at _____ (time). I understand that the Family Week begins at the time of this meeting. During the meeting the level of my freedom and privileges for the week shall be determined by totaling the points earned on the previous Weekly Responsibility Schedule. I agree that parents may change the rules specified in this agreement as they deem necessary. Parental decision is final and argument is inappropriate.

Signed: _____ Date: _____
                        (Kid)

Signed: _____ Signed: _____
                     (Parent)   *(Parent)*

Entitlements to Minors   2

We are fortunate to live in a country where most states grant to each person under the age of eighteen years the following entitlements:

1. A safe home in which to reside
2. Three outfits of season appropriate clothing
3. Nourishing food
4. Medical care
5. A continuing education
6. Reasonable discipline

Rights, Privileges, and Responsibilities

♦ Children:

I shall not take these entitlements for granted, because I realize that only a small percentage of the world's population is equally fortunate. Further, I have dignity, respect, and parental love.

Excess (more than three outfits) or name brand clothing, a private room, use of a telephone, transportation, a T.V., spending money, a stereo, entertainment, trips, etc. are not to be confused with Rights or Entitlements. These are Privileges.

Freedom and other Privileges must be earned in our society through wise choices, appropriate behavior, and consideration for others.

If I am to share in the resources of my home and country, I must accept my share of the responsibilities. It is only through assuming responsibilities and by investing oneself that anyone can ever feel a true sense of belonging.

I have read the above carefully, and I understand the differences between Rights, Entitlements, and Privileges.

Signed: _____   Date _____
               (Kid)

♦ Parental Responsibilities: 3

I/We agree to provide shelter, food, clothing, medical care, opportunity for an education, and reasonable discipline to our child. We love our child enough to say "NO", and to be directed by concern for his or her long range best interest, rather than immediate gratification.

I/We further agree to withold freedom and privileges, until our child has demonstrated readiness for them by wise choices, acceptable behavior, and consideration for others.

I/We want our child to develop self-esteem, and realize that strict compliance with this agreement is important to his or her feelings of self-confidence and self-worth.

I/We agree to attend and conduct the Weekly Family Meeting to be held on _____ (day) at _____ (time). At this time all points on the previous Weekly Responsibility Schedule will be totaled and rank will be adjusted accordingly. In addition, all changes in the Family Agreement and other family business will be announced and discussed.

Signed: _____ Date: _____

(Parent)

Name:_____*Sample*_____   Rank_____   **4**

Date_____ to _____

RESPONSIBILITIES AND EXPECTATIONS

PERSONAL	Points	M	T	W	Th	F	S	Su
General Attitude & Behavior	0-3/day							
Room & Bath clean, uncluttered	0-3/day							
Clothes, clean - cared for	0-3/day							
Personal hygiene showered, hair, teeth)	0-3/day							
Exercise (45 minutes continuous activity - jog, bike, walk, weights, etc.)	0-3/day							
Medication- taken daily, on time	0-3/day							
TOTAL								

Possible Points = 18 per day (6*3) = 126   **Total for week____**

HOME and FAMILY	Points	M	T	W	Th	F	S	Su
Routine daily chores - performed on time and without being reminded (list chores & deadline)	0-3/day							
Considerate and respectful of others	0-3/day							
Avoid arguments - not demanding	0-3/day							
Uses initiative - does extra work without being asked	0-10/wk							
Other assigned chores as needed or requested	0-10/wk							
TOTAL								

Possible Points = 9 per day (3*3) + 20 per week = 83
Total for week____

SCHOOL or WORK	Points	M	T	W	Th	F	S	Su
Attends all classes	0-3/day							
On time for all classes	0-5/wk							
Completed all assignments	0-2/day							
Turned in all assignments	0-2/day							
Participates in school sponsored extracurricular activities	0-10/wk							
TOTAL								

Possible Points = 3 per day + 35 per week = 56
Total for week_____

COMMUNITY	Points	M	T	W	Th	F	S	Su
Attends therapy/support group, positive, attentive, punctual	0-3/day							
Attend church	0-5/wk							
Buy newspaper, stay informed, watch evening news rather than junk t.v.	0-10/wk							
Do community service or volunteer work	0-10/wk							
Has positive attitude towards authority figures	0-3/day							
TOTAL								

Possible Points = 6 per day + 25 per week = 67
Total for week_____

GRAND TOTAL = (___) + (___) + (___) + (___) = _____

FREEDOMS & PRIVILEGES	RANK 1	RANK 2	RANK 3	RANK 4
Total points per week	0-178	179-258	259-288	289-332
Telephone (min. per day)	0	10	30	60
Television (hrs. per day)	0	1 hr/day	2 hr/day	+ 1 unlimited
Stereo - walkman - guitar	0	1 hr/day	1-2 hr/day	unlimited
Time away from home -social occasion	0	4 hrs./week	8 hrs./week	16 hrs. - may include an overnight
Curfew - inside house	No outside activities	8 p.m.	9:00-10:30	11:00
Lights out - in bed	9:00 p.m.	10:00 p.m.	12 midnight	1:30 a.m.
Friend Over	0	0	4 hours	Unlimited
Allowance per week	0	$2.00	$5.00	$10.00

Begin with both parents sitting down together and without frequent interruption. Read through the first page of the Family Agreement. This Statement of Basic Household Rules can be modified very quickly to fit your needs. If ages are similar, house rules may be the same for all of your children. One copy per child will be needed. Each child will be asked for his signature on the first and second page of the agreement. Parents will sign on the first and third page. You may copy the forms in Appendix I for your personal needs.

These are serious, rather absolute laws. A half-truth is a lie! Borrowing something without asking permission is stealing. In fact, many families have found peace by adding , "No borrowing or lending clothes or other possessions" to the list of basic rules. This list should contain only rules which, if violated, result in the imposition of serious consequences or loss of freedoms.

One way many parents deal with a violation of these rules is to automatically reduce freedoms and privileges to the level listed in Rank 1 for a specified number of days. A word of caution, reduction of privileges for much longer than a week often discourages the motivation to work for points during that period of time. Consider imposing an additional consequence to a Rank reduction. For example: Rank 1 for a week, and he must clean the garage to your specification before he can return to an earned Rank.

Lesser matters can easily be dealt with in the body of the Agreement, by the assignment of points to desirable or appropriate behavior. If homework is an issue, give extra weight (more points) to its successful completion and submission. Make up a simple daily check sheet to be signed by the teacher(s), or request weekly incidental grade checks from the school (your child's school counselor can usually arrange this). These sheets must be obtained and submitted to you in order to earn the points for the homework item. This is your child's responsibility. Refrain from reminding him to do homework, hand it in, or have the sheet signed. Usually little or no comment is best. He simply doesn't earn the allotted points for that item, unless and until he has completed the total task.

RESPONSIBILITIES AND EXPECTATIONS

Pages 1 through 3 of the Agreement form its body. We have included sample charts which list responsibilities and privileges many families want. Refer to this sample, which includes a "Point Count" range. Don't worry about the points for the moment.

On blank forms from Appendix I, list the Responsibilities and Expectations for each of your children. We found it convenient to cluster these into four categories: Personal, Home and Family, School or Work, and Community. Neither the categories, nor the number of items are sacred. Modify the forms to fit your needs.

Freedoms and Privileges

Next, list the Freedoms and Privileges that are important to each individual child. Different degrees of each freedom, or amount of each privilege, should be awarded for each Rank or level. Rank 1 should represent little or no freedom or privilege. Rank 4 should represent a maximum allowable level for highly responsible or mature behavior. Ranks 2 and 3 are logical midpoints.

Points and Ranks

The sample Agreement will again prove helpful to you in the next steps. You will decide the point count or point range that seems appropriate for each expectation or responsibility.

Finally, you will assign a range of weekly point totals to each of the four Ranks. The Sample will show how to count the possible points, and to total them. The range of points within each rank can differ from one another. You may want to "play" with the numbers a bit. Remember, you can revise any part of the document, at any time, in order to make it work better. Many families change point counts, after a trial period and you should feel free to do so also even though your teen may protest. Changes need to be initiated and implemented at a family meeting. Revisions should not be made so frequently as to create confusion.

Items may also need updating as your children mature, since the Agreement may be continued until kids age out of the home.

Typically, kids function most of the time back and forth between Ranks 2 and 3. Rank 4 should represent a kind of maturational "stretch". Rank 1 is intended to be quite confining and limiting. It is important that the differences between Ranks be significant enough to motivate a youngster to strive for points and higher Rank.

IMPLEMENTING THE AGREEMENT: CALL A MEETING

As parents, once you are reasonably satisfied with the lists of Responsibilities and Privileges, several copies of the responsibilities set should be made. One set per child, per week will be needed. One Privilege Chart per child is enough, until the chart is changed for whatever reason.

You should also at this time choose a day and time for a weekly family meeting. A weekend time seems to work better for most families. There is less liklihood of conflicts with work and school. Once you have picked a day and time it is important you stick with it. Consistency is part of the formula in making the Family Agreement work.

The final step in initiating the Family Agreement will require that all of the family members who are involved meet and clearly understand the program. The parents should provide each child with a copy of his or her seven page document.

You may begin by giving the children a few moments to quietly look over their packets. It is wise to refuse to address the initial squeals and questions, for the time being. Read each page aloud with the children, making certain that they understand reasonably well. Their understanding of the written program is the objective. Their approval is not necessary. We don't require that they enjoy the new system, only that they participate in it. With some formality, obtain signatures where required.

We recommend starting kids on Rank 2 or Rank 3. Just how well they respond to the whole plan may determine on which of these two levels they will be placed for the first week.

Once in a while we have worked with children who choose not to sign or participate. Calmly explain, "That is fine." If so chosen, they will remain on Rank I with privileges and freedoms accorded that Rank. When they decide to earn greater privileges and freedoms they can demonstrate readiness to become a part of the Family

Agreement.

Sometimes it is useful to have copies of Kids Role and Parents Role, (see Appendix I) handy. Do not get pulled into arguing, defending, or justifying. Speak with calm determination, and show a united parental position. Firmly expect the kids to accept it, because you are the parent. Your attitude will show.

MAINTAINING THE FAMILY AGREEMENT

It will take a few minutes each day to score the sheets. This score sheet should be called to your child's attention each evening. Post the point and privilege charts in an obvious and convenient place. The refrigerator or beside the youngster's bedroom door are locations that have been effective for families with whom we have worked. It is your youngster's responsibility to notify you that he has completed the chore or other activity for which he thinks he has earned points. If he fails to do so he may not receive the points in question.

No arguments are permitted. Parental judgment is final. If the tendency to argue is a problem, simply include a "No argument" line under the Basic Household Rules section.

If your arguments continue then it is time to review Chapter 3 regarding arguments.

Please remember, there will be little incentive for your child to work toward improvement, or for something better, if you are too strict or far too liberal with the points you grant. If your child is making an effort to do what is expected in a timely fashion and with an acceptable attitude he should receive credit.

THE WEEKLY FAMILY MEETING

Once each week, at a given time, the family must routinely meet together. It is during this time that weekly point counts are totaled, and Ranks are established for the following week. (Note: if your family cannot find time to get together for 15 or 20 minutes once a week–you have a very real problem. Sink your teeth into it, and make time!) A time during the weekend works best for most families. There is less conflict with work and school.. It is best if you have predermined what the day and time for the meeting will be before you sit down at your initial meeting. By establishing a weekly family meeting time you communicate to your children that you are serious, and that you intend to get results.

ADVANTAGES

The Family Agreement has multiple purposes and advantages. To list a few:

1. It is consistent with natural and social consequences, which are a part of living in the real world.
2. It clearly defines and communicates expectations, responsibilities, and privileges.
3. It is taken more seriously because it is solemnized by a written, contractual format.
4. It enhances the concepts that privileges are earned, and freedom is a consequence of responsible action.
5. The Family Agreement is self-correcting, thus eliminating the need for imposing consequence after consequence for one unacceptable behavior after another.
6. It helps your child understand that his consequences are a result of his own actions rather than an arbitrary choice made by you as a parent.

The Stick System:
An Alternative To The Family Agreement

Now we would like to discuss an alternative approach to the Family Agreement. The Stick System is simple, more concrete, and especially fun for younger children. It is a kind of token economy, with a bit of an original twist.

Supplies: Craft Sticks
Pen
Stick Container
Behavior/Privilege Charts

When desirable behaviors are positively reinforced (rewarded), they are much more likely to be repeated. Our monitory system is a good example of how people work for a secondary reward (salary or other earnings), in an effort to be able to purchase something which they need or want.

In our society, speeding in a car is undesirable or inappropriate behavior. If we are fined for speeding, we are less likely to repeat speeding behaviors. The fine is a negative reinforcer. We lost the opportunity to purchase something we wanted with the money which we gave up for the fine.

The Stick System is simply a stick economy. Craft sticks are awarded for behaviors which we want to see repeated (appropriate Behaviors). Sticks are broken for behaving inappropriately. Privileges are earned, because they are purchased with unbroken sticks. *Sticks need to be paid or fined as soon as possible following the perfomance of a desirable or undesirable act.*

Craft sticks provide an opportunity for the parent to write on each stick when and how they are earned. Likewise, you may note on the reverse side of the stick when and for what behavior each was "fined" (broken). Broken and whole sticks may be kept for review and discussion.

The child will need a container in which to save his sticks, both the unbroken and the broken. Draw-string pouches, zip-lock plastic bags, and empty cans are among the kinds of containers which have been used successfully as stick banks.

Important: Because purchases are usually made at a later time, this system is also teaching the youngster to *delay immediate gratification in order to work for longer range goals.* This is a critically important lesson, and one which is often inadequately taught in our society.

The number of sticks earned for appropriate behaviors ("wages"), the cost in broken sticks ("fines"), and the prices for valued privileges are all predetermined prior to implementing the system. We have provided you with both sample charts and the blank chart forms (See Appendix I) to make your job easier. Parents are encouraged to change or modify the charts as needed, but any change should be discussed with your teen prior to implementing it.

Privileges may be an object which your child wants to have or to use for a specified period of time, like the TV or telephone, or it may be an opportunity. Opportunities are freedoms, such as staying up 30 minutes later or going out with a friend.

You will need to create something like the following for each individual:

APPROPRIATE BEHAVIORS	# OF STICKS
Make bed each morning as soon as you get up	2
Brush your teeth after breakfast	2
Feed the dog/cat, by 8:00 a.m.	1
Take out the trash	1
Do your homework	4
Get ready for bed, brush teeth	2
Fold clothes	1
Pick up room and put things away by 8:00 p.m.	2
Read a book	2
Vacuum and dust, when asked	3

INAPPROPRIATE BEHAVIORS	# OF STICKS
Arguing	3
Lying	3
Not getting home on time	2
Absent from home without leave	1 per hour
Physical aggression toward people	5
Stealing	3-10
Temper tantrum	1-5
Physical aggression toward objects	3

PRIVILEGE LIST	# OF STICKS
TV time	1 per 1/2 hour
Telephone time	1 per 5 min.
Transportation for social privileges	1-5
Permission for video rental	5
Permission for food treat(pizza, ice cream, soda, candy,etc.)	1-10
Video game time	2 per 1/2 hour
Having a friend over	2 per hour
Going to a friend's house	3 per hour
Having a friend overnight/spending ovenight with a friend	5-10
Recreational time	1 per 1/2 hour

These charts are only examples. Your charts must be customized to fit your household and your kid.

In family therapy sessions, we often ask children to bring in their sticks. Behavior patterns emerge which suggest both the areas in which the youngster is achieving, and areas which may need further work. We review patterns of appropriate behavior and verbally reward growth, and we discuss specific behavioral changes that can help him to avoid futher "fines." Discussing with your child his particular areas of strength or growth provides additional positive verbal reinforcement.

The system works, if you work it! Ideally, there is a specific time at the end of each day when parent(s) and teen sit down together for a few moments. They discuss the behaviors involved in earned and broken sticks. No arguments; parental decisions are final. This is a time to really communicate. Verbal praise should be coupled with the behaviors noted on the earned side of the sticks. Behavior patterns may become evident. It is helpful to develop plans for inhibiting the behaviors associated with broken sticks.

We have worked with several children who, on their own initiative, "read their sticks" over and over to themselves. They take pleasure in feeling good about themselves, for things they have done well. This activity is helpful in developing greater self-discipline, self-control, and self-esteem.

BEADS

From time to time, we have substituted colorful plastic beads for craft sticks. Beads are also readily available where craft supplies are sold.

Beads which have been earned can be strung on a leather thong or string, and warn as a necklace. Some of our preteen youngsters, especially, have placed more value in the beads than in the craft sticks because they do enjoy stringing and wearing them.

SELECTING THE BEST APPROACH

One important feature to be considered in establishing any kind of a positive reinforcement system is the value of the reward(s) selected to your particular child. The value something has is a very individual matter, and values usually change with time. What does your child prefer, at this time in his life?

Beads are the simplest to use, but they lose some important training features. Beads are simply "paid" for performance of an established appropriate behavior. Pre-established inappropriate behaviors will "cost" the child beads. Beads may hold enough value in and of themselves to be adequate for training purposes, or they may be used to purchase privileges, as described above in the section on Sticks.

Craft sticks provide an opportunity for the parent to write on each stick when and how they were earned. Likewise, you may note on the reverse side of the stick when and for what behavior each was "fined" (broken). Broken and whole sticks may be kept for review and discussion.

In family therapy sessions, we often ask children to bring in their sticks. Behavior patterns emerge, which suggest both the areas in which the youngster is achieving, and areas which may need further work. We review patterns of appropriate behavior and verbally reward growth, and we discuss specific behavioral changes that can help him to avoid further "fines". Discussing with your child his particular areas of strength or growth provides additional positive verbal reinforcement.

We have worked with several children who, on their own initiative, "read their sticks" over and over to themselves. They take pleasure in feeling good about themselves, for things they have done well. This activity is helpful in developing greater self-discipline, self-control, and self-esteem.

Throughout this book, but especially throughout this section, we emphasize an important concept: the person is not the same as the behavior. We are NOT what we do!

We love the child. Some of his behaviors are acceptable, but other behaviors are unacceptable. A person may tell a lie, but he is not a lie. The act of telling a lie is a behavior, and the act is unacceptable. The person remains lovable and worthy of respect.

Finally, there is nothing constructive about fault finding, guilt, or blame. They result in defensiveness, hurt, and anger, all of which are obstacles to learning and growth. Blame and guilt are counterproductive to accountability and responsibleness.

CHAPTER 6

USING CONSEQUENCES EFFECTIVELY

Okay, so you have changed what you are doing, vowed to become a more effective parent. How do you know when to use what consequence? Should you reward change to a more positive behavior or should you provide a negative consequence for continuing inappropriate behavior? How can you create consequences that are effective and appropriate for the behavior?

WHAT KIND OF CONSEQUENCES?

Some parents try to change their kids only by providing negative consequences, others by giving only positive consequences. Occasionally, parents express concern over what will happen if they give their child negative consequences. They are concerned their child will be angry and rejecting towards them as parents. True, your child may "not like you" for that particular moment if you impose unpleasant consequences. Kids are good at holding parents emotional hostages when they want their own way. They can make it sound like you have violated the constitution and are giving them "cruel and unusual punishment". Is it okay to give your child or teen unwanted consequences to motivate change? Absolutely.

Negative consequences are part of real life. When your teen is stopped for speeding, the cop is definitely not going to promise him pizza if he will obey the speed limit. He is going to give him a ticket. If your youngster gets caught stealing gum in the grocery store, he will not be given a reward when he promises not to do it again. The sooner your child understands that the consequences of his actions in real life can be negative, the sooner he will be motivated to control his own actions.

As a parent, you are not your child's equal nor his friend. Sometimes your child may say he does not like you, even hates you. It is okay; being a parent is not a popularity contest.

Consider the nature of the behavior when deciding between positive and negative consequences. Do you want to eliminate the behavior in question, or instead, motivate change and improvement? Are you asking your child to stop doing something that he knows very well is unacceptable in your home or the community?

If your teen tries to convince you that he didn't know it was not okay to spit on the floor, trust your instincts. He does know better and any statement he makes to the contrary is just what you think it is: nonsense. In these instances, negative consequences are appropriate.

If, on the other hand, you would like to motivate him to learn to play the piano better, learn a foreign language, keep his room a little neater, or take the trash out more frequently, then providing a positive incentive to do better makes sense.

MAKE THE CONSEQUENCES FIT THE SITUATION

Once you have decided which to do, negative or positive consequences, it is time to design something that fits the situation. Try to imagine what the logical and natural results of your child's actions might be. In an earlier example, we suggested that speeding would result in a ticket. Too many tickets would result in the suspension of your driver's license. After all, reckless driving is immature. So a logical conequence for your teen's irresponsible driving habits might be taking away his car keys and driver's license. Be sure you take the license as well as the keys. A driver's license is a real status symbol with teens, one of new found independence.

If your family is like many, you have the experienced difficulty getting your kid to clean his room. Most kids have too many possessions, and tend to take them for granted. When the room becomes a disaster zone, remove everything (including clothes) that is creating the mess. Place the items in boxes and plastic bags and store them somewhere he cannot get them until he has earned them back through additional chores and responsible behavior. If he can not "find" his treasures for a while, he will learn to value them more and to treat them with greater respect. Being unable to locate his possessions is a logical consequence of a chaotic room.

Should your teen fail to vacuum or do the dishes by a stated deadline, "charge" him for doing it for him. After all, if you are unable to take of your own house cleaning, you have to pay someone to do it for you. So, deduct a reasonable amount from his allowance for the incomplete chore. If he does not receive an allowance deduct the amount from what you had planned to spend on a special treat, trip, new clothes, etc.

When Positive Consequences (Rewards) Are Important

When you would for like your youngster to try a new activity or improve at an old one, it is important to reward the performance of the activity. This is the time to give positive consequences for changing. If you would like for your child to learn to play a musical instrument, provide a positive reward for practicing fifteen minutes twice a day (fifteen minutes twice a day is much more effective than thirty minutes once a day). Agree that he will earn a new tape, CD for his collection, or other appropriate reward if he can meet his practice goal for a stated period of time (perhaps a week for a younger child, 2 weeks for an older child).

If you would like your child to take on extra chores above and beyond the call give him an additional allowance or privilege. After all, if you take on a second job you get paid more. It is a logical consequence for extra effort.

Design Rewards To Fit The Child

For any reward to work (increase the chances that a behavior will be repeated), the reward must have value to the person performing the act. The degree to which something is valued is a highly individual matter. What does your particular teen want, like, or find important?

Consider whether the reward is age appropriate. Does it encourage continued positive behavior? Does the reward have other attributes, such as increased learning (buy a book), social skill development (a trip for a burger with a friend), or family togetherness(a special game time)? Rewards need not be tangible, and should not always be so.

Intangible rewards such as a hug, a special "thank you" or time spent playing a game teach that family, friends and just feeling good about himself are more important than material things. These kinds of rewards encourage children to continue behaving positively.

Tools and strategies for handling specific problem behaviors will be addressed in the next four chapters. Reward new, improved or extra efforts. Do not reward expected behavior.

BE SPECIFIC

Be sure that what ever change you ask of your child can in some way be observed and measured. Otherwise, improvement will be a subjective matter of your kid's word against yours, fertile ground for an argument. For example, if you are asking your child to keep his room cleaner, how are you going to know when that has happened? Be sure you give him a specific description so you will both know when he has acheived his goal and earned his reward. It's very important to give a deadline such as, "..finished by 7:00 o'clock on Saturday evening".

Seldom does anyone get a new skill right on the first try, so, initially, be sure to accept less than perfect attempts. So long as your child tries adequately to reach the established goal, he needs to be rewarded. The standards for rewardable behavior should increase as his skill improves. He will eventually "get it right" if you continue to encourage with rewards of one kind or another. Parental time, acknowledgment, and warm hugs are great rewards for intermediate "successes".

CHAPTER 7

CREATIVE TOOLS FOR PROBLEM BEHAVIOR

After reading the previous six chapters you should have:

1. A basic plan of action for positive, healthy family growth.
2. Guidelines for communicating.
3. Tools, such as the Family Agreement to help create a consistent, responsible environment.
4. Guidelines for using positive and negative consequences.

However, there will still be times when you need to address specific behavior problems. These are the times when you will need to do more then just withhold points on the Agreement.

Gadgets and Gizmos

Most kids do not acquire the ability to think in fully abstract ways until they are well into adolescence. For this reason it may be a challenge to get a younger child to understand why he should not argue, fight, try to "parent the parent", demand constant attention, or otherwise behave inappropriately. For some older kids inappropriate behaviors are so longstanding and automatic that they are unaware of them.

These kids frequently benefit from more experiental learning techniques and from the use of visual aids, which help them learn appropriate behaviors more rapidly. We would like to share with you some of the visual aids which we have found effective in dealing with problem behaviors, behaviors that do not seem to yield to more abstract consequences.

Several of these strategies are humorous in nature, and intended to lighten up an otherwise tense situation. Parental anger and tension are among the greatest of obstacles to the replacement of undesirable behaviors with appropriate behaviors.

At first glance some of these aids may seem humiliating, and your child may protest on those grounds. It is important to point out that the purpose of using these "props" is not humiliation, but increased self-awareness. Use judgement as to when, where, and for how long you use a strategy. It's one thing to wear a Kid Button around the house with only immediate family members present, and quite another to wear it outside the house with a group of peers.

The same old tired approach will, more than likely, result in the same old exhausting results. Based on the belief that if what you're doing is not working well, then it's certainly time to do something different, we will present to you some ideas that have worked quite well for many families.

HANDHELD CASSETTE TAPE RECORDER

Children who are argumentative, demanding, or habitually lie and curse, are frequently impulsive, blaming, loud or sarcastic can benefit from hearing themselves on tape. Kids who have developed these inappropriate habits tend to be unaware of what they are doing. Playing back a taped recording of his tirade is a fast way to put him in touch with reality. The tape recorder is also a handy way of documenting when he has lied or "changed his story."

Your child is likely to try the behaviors we mentioned when it is difficult for you to take action, such as in the car, when you are late for work, or in front of other people. Be prepared and keep the tape recorder with you at all times. It is important to let him know you will not back down under these uncomfortable or inconvenient circumstances.

The tape recorder is powerfully effective in helping kids develop an awareness of their behaviors. In fact, once the child is made aware that he is being recorded, behaviors almost always improve immediately. The child who swears he was not shouting and never said a curse word will suddenly quiet down and speak more respectfully.

When we first suggest using a recorder, we often encounter the objection, "Yes, but he won't argue if he knows that he is being recorded." Exactly! Congratulations! In case this happens, you are already on the road to meeting your objective. Was it not your objective to make him aware of, and to interfere with the habitual response of arguing or cursing loudly? You just did it! You must continue to carry the recorder for a while and to tape his outbursts, if necessary. But he will become undeniably aware of his behavior, and the interference will help break the habit.

If you decide the tape recorder is an intervention you need to use, then begin by letting your child know what you are going to do. A typical announcement to your child might go something like this: "I understand that your don't think you are being loud and demanding or that you are cursing" (of course he knows he is cursing) "so I am going to help you become aware by recording our conversations when I think they are beginning to get out of hand". Your child may respond by immediately indulging in some of the unwanted behaviors, so be prepared and have the recorder handy when you make the announcement.

Many kids will immediately stop doing all those things that they swore they were not doing in the first place. Kids who oppositionally act as if they are unaffected by hearing the tape often "get the message quickly" when they are required to transcribe the tape.

Keep the tape recorder in hand for three or four weeks after the problem dries up. The new and appropriate behavior your child is choosing needs to be positively reinforced. A simple statement like, "I recognize that you are trying to stop being argumentative, and I appreciate it", works nicely.

Do not hesitate to get the recorder out again if or when you think the problem may be returning. Most kids will try old behaviors again when they think you have let down your guard or forgotten. "Just testing the limits, Mom and Dad. Just joking."

DISPOSABLE MASKS

The disposable mask is another tool which helps kids who interrupt, argue or are in other ways verbally inappropriate. Keep a clean one handy and visible. Masks are available at most drug stores, or places where paint and yard chemicals are sold. Let your child know that he will be asked to wear the mask as a reminder not to be verbally inappropriate, argumentative, etc. Put the mask on your child for a stated period of time (10-15 minutes for a younger child, perhaps longer for an older child) and inform him that he will be expected to stay quiet until the mask is removed. If he does not remain silent, the timing will begin again. When you allow your child to remove the mask inform him that the mask will be used any time he becomes verbally inappropriate, in order to help him remember to make the necessary verbal changes.

"HYDRO-THERAPY"

A splash of cool water or a squirt from a spray bottle is a fast and harmless way of getting the attention of a child who is arguing, throwing a temper tantrum, cursing, fighting with a sibling or who will not get out of bed in the morning.

A clean spray bottle with cold water is one way. We suggest you choose a bottle with an adjustable nozzle that will shoot a concentrated stream of water four to five feet. Be sure to use a clean bottle that has never contained any type of chemical solution (NOTE: even a bottle that has been thoroughly washed can still retain harmful residues of some insecticides or other chemicals). Keep the bottle full of clean, cool water. You can even store the bottle in plain view at the front of the refrigerator! It helps as a deterrent.

Water serves two purposes in these situations. First, it brings to your child's attention that he is doing something that is unacceptable. He can then shift his attention to listening to your instructions. Secondly, the water interrupts the inappropriate behavioral sequence, and prevents its completion. It is therefore less likely to be repeated.

If your child throws a fit when you douse him, let him know that he will receive further "hydrotherapy" or other consequences if the tantrum does not stop immediately.

GLOVES

Use gloves (any kind will do) for kids who take things that do not belong to them. Inform the child he will be expected to wear the gloves for a specific length of time, to be determined by you, each time he takes something that is not his. Rubber gloves are especially good for sticky fingers.

Boxing gloves are great for kids who punch things like the wall, a door, a brother, etc. An old duffel bag, stuffed with sphagnum moss, and hung securely from a tree or a garage beam makes an inexpensive punching bag to appropriately substitute for something or someone else.

"Kid" and "Parent" Buttons

Kids who try to tell their parents what to do are playing the parent role. Help a child to remember his own role by giving him a "Kid" button to wear; you may even ask him to write the twelve items listed under "Kid Role" in Appendix I.

His awareness may be further increased by wearing a button yourself that says "Parent". Let your child know he will be expected to wear his "Kid" button until he can remember on his own to behave like a kid.

Buttons can be created easily from a round of stiff cardboard, a safety pin and some heavy tape. You may prefer to buy a package of name tags that say, "Hello, I am...the kid.......or anything else he needs to be reminded to change.

"PUSH" BUTTONS

If you have a child who easily escalates himself into temper tantrums or out of control behavior when others do things to displease him, then give him the "Push" button to wear. The "Push" button is to remind him that he is letting others "push his buttons". Now is a good time to explain to your child that he is in charge of how he feels. He can choose to react appropriately or to overreact.

The "Push" button is a good reminder for siblings who like to tease each other. Your kids need to understand that trying to push another kid's buttons or letting their own buttons get pushed is inappropriate. Kids who push buttons are manipulating and playing power games. Kids who let their buttons get pushed are giving away their power and trying to give responsibility for their feelings to others.

MARBLES

We strongly believe that any child over the age of eight or nine should learn to be responsible for getting himself up in the morning with the use of an alarm clock. Not only does this help avoid some potential problems, it is a good means of becoming increasingly self-reliant. Self-reliance is an important factor in the development of self-esteem.

If you are having trouble getting your child out of bed, some of our parents informed us that a bag of marbles kept in the freezer work wonders! If your child has not gotten up on time, dump the bag of cold marbles under his covers. They have a tendency to roll to the center of the bed where he is snoozing!

The message is: have fun with these things. Not becoming too serious can lower parental frustration levels and help to prevent parents from verbal or physical child abuse.

Reminder Bracelets

This is a step up from the old string-around-the-finger technique. For some kids, "I forgot" seems to be the response to any obligation, chore, or homework that they do not like. Help his poor "memory" by giving him a reminder bracelet to wear, until he takes care of the specific request and learns to be responsible. Let him know that he may choose to wear the bracelet until you remove it, or he will have automatically chosen a more severe consequence.

We use the type of I.D. bracelets issued to hospital patients, purchased inexpensively from a medical supply store. We like the hospital bracelets because there is a place to insert a message. We write in that space the item or chore to be remembered. Many other things you can devise will work as well. A strip cut from a plastic bottle, marked with a permanent marker, and taped together will do.

Kids will suddenly develop better "memories" when their friends start asking why they are wearing that strange bracelet. Explaining to friends is definitely not "cool". We've seen kids wear a long sleeve shirt in the summer to cover the bracelet, but that's hardly abusive. Becoming more responsible is well worth it.

Spray Room Deodorizers

Spray room deodorizers are a dramatic solution for the child who will not take care of his personal hygiene. Spray the air around him liberally every time he enters the room, and announce loudly that the practice will continue until he learns to change clothes, shampoo his hair, shower and use deodorant on a daily basis. Embarrassing? So is body odor!

In addition, you may use liberal amounts of inexpensive, very sweet cologne on the kid.

DENTAL DISCLOSURE TABLETS

The little red tablets you buy at the drug store to reveal plaque on tooth enamel are a good tool for a child who will not brush, especially those who wear braces. When he says he has brushed and you suspect he has not, because only fifteen seconds elapsed between the time you said "brush" and he said "finished", ask him to chew one of the little tablets and see what turns red!

FOR MORE SPECIFIC SOLUTIONS...

Finally, we suggest that you turn to Appendix II, wherein we address many specific behaviors that parents encounter. They are listed in alphabetical order according to the subject. Solutions are provided *and* appropriate parental responses are also included.

CHAPTER 8

HOW TO USE WRITING ASSIGNMENTS

Most parents have had the experience of saying to a child "Why did you do that?", and getting the answer, "I dunno" or "I forgot." In most cases, your child will not know why he behaved the way he did. "Why?" simply creates frustration for both you and your child, and is usually a question best avoided.

Your child may have actually forgotten to take care of the task in question. He may be resisting passively, in the belief that there will be no consequences. Whatever the case, writing assignments are an effective consequence for your child. If he did actually "forget" or does not really "know", he needs to learn responsibility and to understand "why". Writing assignments are a good tool for this task.

Writing, the act of putting into words your thoughts and feelings about a specific question or issue, is a very effective means of defining the problem. When kids have to spend time and effort thinking about a problem, they begin to develop a better awareness of their actions. Awareness is the first step to change.

In addition, for the passive resistant child, writing assignments serve the function of providing appropriate consequences for the irresponsible behavior. There is also a strong tendency for a kid to suddenly "find his tongue" and converse with you when offered a choice such as, "Tell me about it or write a couple of pages of explanation".

Writing assignments help your child improve his writing, grammar and spelling skills. All assignments he turns in to you should be corrected for clear and responsible thinking, grammar, spelling and neatness. They may then be returned to him for rewriting. Reviewing the writing assignments will also keep you abreast of your child's academic level.

BACK TO BASICS

How do you choose appropriate topics for writing assignments? Pick topics which are relevant to the behavior problem, and which will provide a learning experience.

SENSIBLE SENTENCES

Remember when you had to write on the board one hundred times, "I will not chew gum in class?" A new tack on the "sentence-on-the-board-after-school" approach is the "sensible sentence" consequence. The big difference between the "sensible sentence" and sentence writing is the positive approach we take. Traditionally, sentences on the blackboard have emphasized what kids should not do. We use "sensible sentences" to emphasize what the child should be doing......and thinking.

We suggest picking a positive statement which emphasizes what your child should be doing to act responsibly, written a reasonable number of times for his age and level of academic maturity. For example, we have recently worked with a youngster who "frequently forgot to tell the truth". An effective "sensible sentence" for him has been "Honesty is the key to responsible living." The first time this youngster was caught in a lie she wrote the "sensible sentence" fifty times. The second time she was caught she wrote the sentence seventy five times. Each lie increased the assignment by twenty five repetitions.

For those children who learn best through concrete assignments and repetition , "sensible sentences" may be an answer.

PRODUCTIVE PARAGRAPHS

A variation on the "sensible sentence" approach is an intervention we call the "productive paragraph". Again, thinking enough about the problem is the key to change.

For older kids, or for kids who have done "sensible sentences" previously, "productive paragraphs" may be a better consequence and can be implemented in a similar manner.

At the end of the chapter are examples of sentences and paragraphs that we use regularly. Feel free to design your own or customize ours to fit your situation.

By now you know that your child is capable of endless creativity. Put his creativity to work as a learning experience when you encounter verbal resistance to your questions.

CONSTRUCTIVE COMPOSITIONS

How many times have you asked a simple and appropriate question only to encounter the response, "I dunno", "I forgot", "nothin" or simply receive a vacant stare? Constructive compositions may be a good consequence. You can offer choices, thereby preventing increased resistance.

You may make a statement such as, "I find it confusing when you respond that way; if you do not choose to explain orally you may write an explanation on paper." This example is a good remedy for a bad case of the "I dunno's, "I forgot's" and particularly the blank stares.

If your child does not respond within a few seconds, quietly and unemotionally state "I see you have chosen to write out the explanation." Your child may respond, "but I can't think of an explanation". If this is the response you receive then you need only say, "Then writing will help you think."

Putting your thoughts and feelings into words is an effective way of thinking through the problem and defining it. Problem definition aids in awareness and is frequently the first step in solving the problem.

SAMPLE PRESCRIPTIVE WRITING ASSIGNMENTS

Sensible sentences:

1. When your child is demanding, tries to tell you what to do:
   It is not my job to parent my parents.
2. When he blames others for his feelings: I am responsible for my feelings, attitude, behavior, and their consequences.
3. When he says "but so and so did it too": I cannot change others, but I can change myself.

4. When he refuses to do chores not involving his own room, clothes, says "I never use that part of the house", etc: I share my family resources, therefore I must share in the responsibilities.

5. When he tries to push other people's buttons: I shall develop self-control, rather than attempting to control other people.

6. When he lies or acts in an untrustworthy fashion: I shall become reliable, because trust is extremely important.

7. When he is rude, disrespectful: I shall learn to be considerate and respectful of others.

8. When he lies either by comission or omission: Lying causes more problems than it solves.

9. When he "forgets": If I can remember to do things that are important to me, I can remember to do things that I am asked to do.

10. When he needs to understand we must all do things we do not like: Not wanting to do something simply is not reason enough to fail to do it.

11. When he confuses rights and privileges: Wanting some thing does not mean that I deserve it, or that I am entitled to it.

12. When he needs to learn to delay gratification: I can learn to wait and to work for something that is important to me.

Productive Paragraphs:

1. When your child blames others for his thoughts or feelings: When I refuse to take responsibility for my thoughts, feelings, or actions, I am giving away my appropriate power. It is no wonder that I feel powerless, and controlled by other people or situations. Feeling controlled and powerless is most uncomfortable, and I feel inadequate-like a nothing or a nobody. Those are the times when I inappropriately attempt to control everybody and everything. By

taking responsibility for my thoughts, feelings, actions, and for their consequences, I can avoid all of this misery, and become a very real person.

2. When your child confuses his rights with his privileges: Because I am fortunate enough to live in this country, I am entitled to :
(1) A safe home in which to reside
(2) Three outfits of season appropriate clothing
(3) Nourishing food
(4) Medical care
(5) A continuing education
(6) Reasonable discipline

Most children in the world do not have these things, so I shall not take them for granted. These six entitlements are my rights. Everything else is a privilege, and privileges are earned by responsible attitudes, beliefs, and behaviors.

3. When your child does not want to help out with chores, claims he does not use anything and should not have to clean it up: If I am to share in the resources of my home and my country, I must accept my share of the responsibilities. It is only through assuming responsibilities and by investing onself, that anyone can ever feel a true sense of belonging. A feeling of belonging is important to a healthy, happy person. Therefore, I shall invest myself in my home and my society by contributing my fair share. I shall give to them, as well as take from them. As a natural consequence, I will feel much better about myself.

4. For kids who have difficulty accepting they make mistakes: It is O.K. for me to make mistakes, and it is O.K. for other people to make mistakes. Making mistakes is a part of being human. I need only to own my errors, and to learn from them. Mistakes do not make us bad people. Instead, they can become constructive opportunities for growth and maturity.

5. For kids who blame others for their problems: Fault-finding and blame-games are unnecessary and usually distructive. Faulting and blaming self or others are defensive and contagious. We can live responsibly and accountably without guilt trips. No-fault living is perfectly possible if we defocus from the sins and the sinners, and concentrate on the solutions to defined problems.

6. For the child who is overdramatic, blows situations out of proportion: Real pleasures in life come from personal growth and healthy relationships with other people. Creating crises, and contriving excitement in my life are phoney attempts to get attention, and to defocus from the hard work of improving oneself and/or ones' relationship with others. Leave phoney crises and excitement to the Soap Opras, and concentrate on personal growth and development.

7. For the child who tries to focus on other peoples faults instead of his own: I will not try to change others. I am not responsible for the behaviors of others. I will work to change my own thoughts, feelings, and actions. The behaviors of others may be influenced by the changes in me, but that is up to the other person.

8. To help a child take responsibility for his own actions, thoughts and feelings: It may take some work, but I can change the things that I do, think, and feel. That is a wonderful part of being human. I can start by either thinking differently about something, or by acting differently toward it.

9. For the child who confuses inability to tolerate discomfort with unwillingness to tolerate it: When I tell myself or others that something is terrible and that "I can't stand it", I throw away some of my self-confidence. Self-confidence is based on the realistic belief that I can cope or deal with problems. What I really mean is, "I don't want it".

10. For the child who will not try to change: It is foolish to keep doing the same thing over and over, and to expect that the results will be different. If I remain aware of what I am doing, and open my mind to other possibilities, I can make different choices and take a different approach.

Constructive Compositions

Instruction: "We often learn a great deal by writing. Please write ____ (1-5) pages or more on the subject of _____
_____.

1. For the child who answers "I dunno" a lot, or does not seem to know what he wants: What do I value? (Or, what is important to me?)

2. For the child who demands things/privileges he has not earned: The difference between Rights and Privileges

3. For a child who uses an inappropriate tone of voice, refuses eye contact, wears inappropriate clothing, or acts flirtatiously: What messages do I send with my body language?

4. For the child who says "I'll do it later" but never does: What is procrastination ?

5. For the child who "forgets", says "I dunno": What messages do I send when I resisting by passive behavior

6. For the child who makes poor choices about friends, dress, etc: What messages do I send to others with my_____ ? (dress, choice of music, language, choice of friends, etc.)

7. For a child who has no plans for the future or who wants to drop out of school, live on his own, etc: What are my goals, and how do I plan to achieve them?

8. For a child whose behavior is irresponsible or untrustworthy: Why is responsible behavior important?

9. For the child who takes risks, gets involved in dangerous behavior such as drugs, indiscriminate sex, hanging out with friends who take risks: How is your behavior self-destructive?

10. For a child who cannot separate his behavior from self, and thinks of himself as "bad": What is the difference between the person and his behavior?

11. For the child who blames others for his actions, thoughts and feelings: Owning my thoughts, feelings, behaviors, and their consequences is responsible living. What does it say about me?

12. For a child who is rude, argumentative, sarcastic: Why is it important to show respect for others (or, be considerate of others) and how can I do that?

CHAPTER 9

PROBLEMS DESERVING
SPECIAL ATTENTION

There are some significant situations that we have not addressed, and that deserve special attention. These situations include hitting(and fighting), lying, stealing, running away and sexual acting out. These behaviors can be the symptom of a more serious problem.We will look at them individually.

"BUT HE HIT ME FIRST"

We hear an ever increasing number of kids today in family and group peer therapy talk about encountering physical aggression in school and community. Adolescents and pre-adolescents generally sight one of three reasons for striking or otherwise employing physical aggression towards a peer, classmate, or sibling: 1) *"He hit me first."* 2) *"If I hit him back he'll find out he can't get away with it"*. 3) *"I have to defend myself or else I'll get beaten up."* Physical aggression encountered on the way to school, at school, both inside and on the playground or campus has become a bigger problem than many school faculties can handle, or choose to handle. So what does your child do when a another child strikes him, shoves him or otherwise challenges him to fight and no authority is in sight to intervene?

"It Isn't Fair"

First of all, most elementary school age kids are keen on everything being "fair", so retaliating in kind, an "eye for an eye" so to speak, makes sense to them. When your child says "he hit me first" he is telling you he thinks this is a fair solution. But the real message is that it is okay to solve his problems by doing something he resents being done to him.

It is also important to understand fighting only perpetuates the cycle of aggression. Many kids believe that hitting a kid back teaches other kids to leave him alone. There may be cases where that is true, but in most instances it only reinforces the aggressor's belief in hitting and also signals that he can "push" your child's "buttons". Kids who are successful at "button pushing" usually come back for more. After all, it is good entertainment, and they get the same "rush" they get when pushing an adult's buttons. Some kids like to use name calling and teasing to challenge a peer to fight a third child. They get entertained while their peers pay the price in detention or through other consequences.

If your child blames the teacher or faculty for not handling the problem, argues he has no choice but to defend himself, keep in mind he will not always have an authority figure available to intervene. He needs to learn how to handle his own conflicts. So, how can you convince your child there are better ways of handling confrontation?

HELPING YOUR CHILD CHANGE

First, keep in mind that a person who responds to an invitation to fight feels powerless and sees fighting as a way of regaining lost power. Let your child know you understand that he is feeling powerless, but there are better ways to change that feeling.

Remind him that fighting is another way of competing. Assure him he does not have to "win" to be okay. When he hits back he may think he is sending an "I win" message. The real message to other kids is that he is okay with hitting, not that he does not like being hit. Ask him to practice using "I feel statements" (see Chapter 4, How To Speak The Same Language As Your Child)to tell his opponent what he does not like.

Second, emphasize what really happens when your child fights is that he is being controlled by other kids. They are using him for entertainment. Ask your child if he wants to be manipulated by others. Point out to him that by getting into a fight he is doing just what the other kid wants and in the process ensuring they will come back for more.

Ask your child to imagine what it would be like to be a puppet on a string. Explain that every time someone teases him or calls him a name, he is allowing his "strings to be pulled". Point out that real power is choosing not to be pulled into a fight.

Explain to your child that he keeps his power when he chooses to do what the other child is not expecting, such as smiling and saying "no thank you, I'm not interested in being your entertainment."He may choose to walk away or go to a teacher or other authority figure and ask for help.

It is important to emphasize to your child that kids who are looking for a fight will go somewhere else to pick them, if he does not respond. There is no reward in being ignored and if your child will hang in there and ignore the aggressor long enough, he will give up because he gets bored. It is a little like putting a blank tape in the VCR. How long will anyone watch a blank tape?

If your child is good at being passive resistant(see Chapter 11, Power Battles) here is one challenge where he can channel an otherwise problem behavior into something positive. Suggest to your child that he can "forget" to meet the other kid for the showdown or pretend he does not understand what the aggressor wants. Help your child to imagine the frustration of the aggressor when he "forgets". Emphasize the powerful way he will feel if he channels his passive aggression positively.

Third, if you are hearing that it is impossible to avoid fighting at school, look for patterns in the stories your child tells. Does the problem always seem to happen in the same place, with the same child or at the same time? It is also important to ask your child to examine his own behavior. Are there any ways your child invites a fight? Is he name calling, staring, making gestures, talking about the another child behind his back, putting him down verbally? It is important to ask about these details. If he is getting into fights frequently, it is just possible he is "forgetting" to tell you all of the story.

If none of these tactics work, it is time to visit with your child's teachers and counselor to determine if there is enough supervision by adults and to be sure that your are getting the full story.

Sibling Rivalry

Fighting at home with siblings is another arena with the same or similar motives as school fighting. Siblings often compete, with the reward being "power", attention from you the parent or, frequently, just for entertainment. You can apply the same logic and because the conflict is happening at home, provide a wider range of consequences and interventions.

BUTTON PUSHING

If a younger child seems to be constantly the "victim" of his older siblings teasing and harrassment, ask him if he likes being his sister's or brother's entertainment and give him a button or tag(see Chapter 7, Creative Tools for Problem Behavior) to wear that says "PUSH" . Let your child know that every time he lets his older sibling get him angry he has allowed his button to be "pushed". When he begins to ignore his sibling, tell him he can put a black or red bar made from ribbon or tape across the button or tag to indicate he no longer tolerates his sibling's behavior.

For older siblings who tease younger ones, have a talk about the "time they seem to have on their hands." After all, if they have time to tease a sibling they "probably do not have enough to do". Assign extra chores to "keep them busy". Remind them that if they continue to find they have time for teasing you will continue to find more chores to "keep them busy".

Sibling fighting is another place where water can be helpful. When you find your children beginning to get physically aggressive with one another, give them each a good splash. Splashing a glass of water on them has several benefits: 1) Your kids will be distracted and forget the reason for the fight 2)The shock of the cold water will get you their immediate attention, 3) The cold water will help them to calm down, and the cycle of fighting will not be completed, helping to break the habit.

Once you have your kids attention ask them to discuss the reason for the conflict without making accusations. That means they each need to talk about their own needs and avoid blaming their sibling(ask them to make statements that include the pronoun "I" and avoid the pronoun "you"). Coach both siblings in making an "I feel" statement to the other and encourage them to work out a compromise where each will get something he wants. You may want to review Chapter 4, How To Speak the Same Language as Your Child.

Once they have been coached in learning to compromise and resolve their own conflicts, resist the temptation to jump in immediately and resolve the conflict for them. Kids need opportunities to practice learning to resolve their own conflicts. If we always jump in and take care of it, they will never learn how and will continue to escalate any disagreement into a fight.

The time to jump in is when you are hearing signals the conflict is about to become physical. Get their attention and let them know they must come up with a peaceful solution, use the skills you have taught them, or you will provide a solution they may not like. It is important to keep in mind that if the solutions you provide when they fight are always ones your kids enjoy, there may be no incentive to try and resolve their own differences. A negative consequence for both kids should be provided if you have to resolve the problem. Writing assignments can be useful.

IS YOUR CHILD REALLY REALLY LOOKING FOR ATTENTION?

Some children will continue to drag out their conflicts even after parental interventions. It may be they are really asking for your intervention or attention. Let them know that such tactics are an inappropriate way of asking for attention and they must resolve their own conflicts. If they need your attention they must ask for it appropriately.

THE AGGRESSIVE TEEN

In working with families of adolescents, we occasionally hear parents express concern about their teenager becoming aggressive.

Sometimes the concern is about aggression towards objects, such as a teen who becomes angry and punches a hole in his door. Sometimes the aggression is expressed towards the parent or a sibling with whom he disagrees.

TOO MUCH TO HANDLE

How will you know when the aggression is too much handle? If it tends to escalate until the child is out of control it is probably getting dangerous. It may start with verbal aggression but grow into displays of physical aggression. Your child may throw a shoe at you or shove you. Right now, it may not seem significant but as your teen grows physically the aggression becomes much more dangerous.

Anger is a legitimate feeling, and should be accepted as such in ourselves and in others. Although it is fine to feel angry, it's not okay to respond to the feeling by violence to persons nor with destruction to property.

People with low tolerance to frustration experience anger more frequently than do others, and may react with more violence and aggression. Tolerance to frustration and alternatives to aggression are learned, and we must teach them to our children.

Anger and fear stimulate the body to produce adrenaline, a kind of "super-fuel". Adrenaline can be worked off in a constructive manner, such as exercise, as well as in destructive or violent ways. It's a personal decision, and our kids should learn that they have numerous choices from which to select a response.

A teen may be beyond parental control, if he has not learned to explore feelings of hurt, fear, and frustration, and to deal appropriately with anger before he is physically large and strong. Inappropriate power and control issues further complicate the situation.

Society holds parents responsible for their children. We have worked with parents, especially single mothers, who are realistically fearful of their out-of-control kid. Recognizing that they cannot be responsible for children over whom they have no control, these parents sought professional help.

If your teen is aggressive, strong, and out of control, do not put yourself or others at risk. Get professional help now.

HONESTY, DECEPTION, AND LIES

Being aware of what is happening around us, interpreting those events realistically, and being open and honest with others comprise the foundation of good mental health and good relationships.

Without honesty, we cannot experience validation of the real self. Without validation, it is unlikely a person can accept himself as a good and worthwhile person. Self-esteem is impossible without self acceptance.

When we are dishonest or deceptive, we can only conclude that we are reasonably good manipulators. We can gain no feedback as to whether or not the real person is acceptable and of worth to self or others. It is notable here that we can be deceptive to ourselves and/or to others. Certainly self-deception is the most destructive and self-defeating of all.

Honesty is the characteristic most often reported to us by adolescents as a "highly valued" personal characteristic. So, why does "dishonesty" or "frequent lying" top their parent's list of behaviors that they would like for their kids to change?

WHEN IS A LIE A LIE?

It is deceptive, and therefore a lie, anytime we intentionally send a message which is untrue to ourselves or to another person.

Again, self-deception is especially malignant.

We are responsible for clarifying any message that we realize has been incorrectly interpreted by another person. To mislead another by what we refrain from saying is a deception. A half-truth is a lie. Thus, there are lies of omission, and lies of commission.

If we are doing our best to live openly and honestly, there is simply no reason to lie. It's O.K. to be imperfect, and to make mistakes from time to time. It is much healthier, and far less painful in the long run, to accept responsibility for the consequences of our choices than it is to try to deceive ourselves or others. We develop self-confidence by learning that we can tolerate the consequences of our behaviors.

The importance of modeling and teaching these concepts to our children cannot be overstated

CHANGING DISHONEST BEHAVIOR

It's unnecessary to determine the motives behind most behaviors, in order to significantly change them. In general, this holds true for lying and deceptiveness as well. A person who tends to lie about most anything probably fails to adequately value truth and trustworthiness. Lying is mindless, and a habit.

Connie, age thirteen, fell into this habitual category. Her parents were extremely frustrated by this behavior, and exclaimed in desperation that they had "tried everything". The therapist realized that their level of concern was so great that they must "lighten up" in order to successfully resolve the problem. They were so overfocused on their daughter's deceptions, that she could control her parent's emotions and gain excessive attention by lying.

The therapist prescribed "turning the table" for a week, and advised the parents to "have some fun with it." Connie's parents, a bit reluctant at first, rapidly got into the spirit of the prescribed treatment. "Sure, I washed your favorite jeans for school today. I can't imagine how they got back in the dirty clothes", "Money for the movies? When did I say that?", "Where did you get the idea I would pick you up from school today?", "Why, I was home all day". And so it went for a week.

Because a much overworked, " I forgot" can also be a deceptive excuse for the more honest response, "I didn't want to", these parents "forgot" to do a number of things. Mom "forgot" to prepare dinner one night. Dad "forgot" to pick up a favorite soft-drink on his way home from work.. After a few days of confusion, this young lady begin to get the message. A trust base is very important to our relationships.

In order to change dishonest behavior, responsible adults must themselves be deeply committed to the truth. When children ask questions that are appropriately of no concern to them, they should be told just that. " This is really not of concern to you" beats a lie every time. Actually, this rule holds true for persons of any age.

The role of a child, and the role of a parent or adult in authority are different. What a youngster is doing is most often of concern to the parent, as supervision and child rearing are parental responsibilities. Failure to inform you of something that you need to be told, minimizing or exaggerating, or in any other way purposefully misleading you is dishonest, unacceptable, and often dangerous.

Avoid games or tricks to "catch him in a lie". Such a set-up is also dishonest. At the same time, when dealing with your child, refuse to be sidetracked or derailed. Stay focused on the issue at hand.

THE WHY BEHIND THE LIE

Sometimes it may be helpful to determine the "why" behind the lie, in order to better develop strategies for dealing with the behavior. Purposefully dishonest behavior can occur because of an underlying belief system held by the child. When uncovered, these belief systems are invariably untrue and unhealthy.

These are possible beliefs which may lead to chronic lying:

1. Exaggerating the events in my life makes me seem important or exciting.
2. Being imperfect is unacceptable.
3. I must be number one at everything I do in order to be valued by myself and others.
4. Someone or something else is responsible for my behavior-"they made me do it."
5. "I cannot tolerate the consequences of my behavior."
6. "I should not have to tolerate the consequences of my behavior."
7. "I want it (or don't want it) and therefore I should have my way. That's reason enough to lie."
8. "Conflict is intolerable to me, and I must avoid it at all costs."

Becoming aware of a pattern or patterns of lies can be useful. In these cases, assisting the youngster to understand that these underlying beliefs are false can expedite changing the behavior of lying. Writing assignments(See Chapter 8, Writing Assignments) are a good way of helping a child who holds one of these false beliefs.

.

"I Can Make It On My Own"

The heading of this section illustrates a response frequently heard by parents of adolescents who are threatening to run away. Adolescents are going through the painful struggle of figuring out who they really are. That almost always means trying to be different from their parents and families.

Sometimes they equate living by your rules as being like you. So getting into a power struggle about rules may be seen as necessary, if he is to be an individual. How do they communicate that? Sometimes by telling you that you are out of touch with the times. And, sometimes by saying they can make it on their own and showing you they can by running away.

Threatening to run away is a tactic designed to get you to back off and let them make their own rules. Stand your ground. It is your home and you set the rules. What do you say when kids threaten to run away? It is important to make it clear what action you will take if they should run away, and to also make it clear that you understand they disagree with you and may not find your rules logical. A statement like this is appropriate: "I hear that you don't like our rules or think that they make sense. That's okay. If you choose to live in our family you must still obey them. When you can show by your actions that you are exercising good judgement, then we can talk about changing the rules."

You should also make clear to your teen what action you will take if he does run away. He needs to know that there will be consequences if chooses to act in this irresponsible manner.

The first time he runs away you should make it clear that he has shown you by his actions he cannot be trusted. You can send this message to your teen by requiring that he check in all of his shoes with you until he proves his trustworthiness. If it is winter time your can also have him check in his coat.

If he ran away with friends or hid out with them, inform him that those friends will be off limits until you decide differently. The following statement is appropriate: "Since you seem unable to make good decisions, when in the company of _____, you may not associate with them until I decide otherwise." The consequences described above should be kept in force until your teen's attitude and behavior indicate that he can be trusted.

Take a snap shot of him if you have no recent photograph. A 5 X 7 school picture is perfect. Explain that you will use it to make posters which you will place at all of his hangouts if he runs away again. The poster should list your phone number and request that the reader call if he has seen your teen. You might also want to mention that providing him with a hiding place is illegal. An example of such a poster is on the following page. You should also maintain a list of your teen's friends and their home phone numbers, parents' names, etc. They will be the first places you should contact when you suspect that your teen has run away. This list will also be helpful to the police if your have to call them. Keep the list where your teen cannot find it.

You should also mention to your teen that the photo will be given to the police when you file a run-away order. Make it clear that you will do this and explain the legal penalties that will follow. Your teen may be required to go to court, do community service etc., if he is picked up by the police for running away.

If your teen calls home while A.W.O.L. and tries to bargain with you or agrees to come home if you change the rules, stand your ground. Make it clear that you want him to come home but he must live by your rules. You will change them only when appropriate and when he is acting responsibly enough to handle different rules. If he still refuses to live by your rules then let him know that you are comfortable with him spending a few nights in the local shelter until he decides he can live by your rules. Have the number and address of the shelter handy for him. Remind him that if he is staying with friends he puts them in the position of breaking the law for harboring a minor.

If your teen continues to run away after you have tried these solutions, then it is time to seek professional help.

HAVE YOU SEEN THIS PERSON?

CALL 000-0000
If You Know Where He Is

Description:

Note: Please be aware that harboring a minor in your home is against the law!

GREEN HAIR AND NOSE RINGS

Earlier we talked about your teenager's need to prove that he is different than you and the rest of his family. Frequently teenagers attempt to prove it to themselves and others by adopting bizarre clothing styles. Teenagers also may pick outrageous clothes, jewelry and hairstyles when they are in power battles with parents and other authority figures. "Belonging" or 'identity" with a peer group and attention-getting are also possible motives.

If your teen has been successful in the past at "pushing your buttons" and clothing or appearance are important to you, watch out! Green hair, or some other look from another planet, may be another attempt to push your buttons and get you into a power struggle. We recommend you choose not to play this game.

Rather than telling him your opinion about his appearance, let logical consequences take their course. If your teen has been wanting a job, now is the time to let him apply for one. When he does not succeed, ask him why he thinks he is having difficulty.

If he gets an infection from the pierced belly button, let him go to a public clinic for treatment ("If you are going to make poor decisions about your health, then you must deal with the consequences yourself"). He needs to know that you will not pay for his poor decision making.

GANG WEAR

If your teen's clothing and hairstyle choices extend to gang symbols, it is time to draw the line. Wearing gang haircuts, clothing or colors can get your teen hurt or killed in some cities. Now is a good time for a writing assignments such as Constructive Compositions #6 and #9 found on page 78. Be sure and discuss the results with your teen and tell him what messages you get from his dress, etc. If he refuses to accept your opinions, then give him an additional assignment to "interview" a teacher, counselor or other school authority. Assign him ask them what message they think is sent by gang wear. In addition, assign your teen to interview half a dozen of his peers who are responsible and doing well in school(pick kids who are active in extracurricular school activities, hold school offices, etc.) and discuss the results of these "interviews".

If your teen continues to resist change, then it is time to take more serious action. Call a meeting. Offer your teen a choice: give him a stated period of time to change his appearance or you will provide consequences. If he does not respond appropriately, confiscate the clothes, initiate the Family Agreement, and/or accompany him on any activities outside the home.

TEENS AND SEX

The increase in sexual activity in teens today is one of the ways in which their generation is significantly different than their parents. Sure, teens of thirty years ago were pressured to have sex and did get sexually involved. There are some differences however. The last generation was not exposed to blatant displays of sexuality on televison and in the movies. This exposure has insidiously sent the message that sex at an early age and sex outside of marriage is okay. Rarely does television or the movies portray the reality of teen pregnancy and HIV infection. Teens today are also mobile at an earlier age and less likely to be under adult supervsion. They have more opportunity for sexual activity and at an earlier age.

If your teen insists that his or her partner is a virgin, encourage tests to prove lack of infection. A sexual partner who is a virgin should have no problem with proving him or herself to be infection free.

Further, see that your sexually active teen has frequent periodic checks at a public clinic. Blood tests do not reveal all types of sexually transmitted diseases. A complete check-up is indicated. We understand that he finds these check-ups distasteful, but they are a logical, socially responsible consequence of his choice to be sexually active.

BIRTH CONTROL AND SEX EDUCATION

What can you do to increase the chances that your teen will make good choices about sexual activity? The key is education. Most kids still get alot of their sex education from peers. Adolescents, as a result of their developmental stage, also tend to think of themselves as "bullet proof". Accidents, death, and disease are things that happen to other people, so far as your teen is concerned. Being sure that your teen is informed is your responsibility as a parent.

IS IT OKAY TO PROVIDE BIRTH CONTROL?

Before we go any further, let us dispel the myth that providing birth control and sex education is the same as "giving your child license" to be sexually active. If he becomes sexually active he will be "driving without a license" anyway! Education will help make him aware of the risks he is taking and how he can best protect himself. Birth control can help safeguard him against disease and protect his future. You can still say, "I don't approve of your choice to be sexually active at your age, but if you choose to be, know what risks you are taking and guard against them".

By providing your teen with sex education you also ensure that he is accurately informed. Kids begin picking up information at an early age, and it is often inaccurate. Many teens believe a condom will protect them from HIV infection. Others may think they or their partner could not possibly have a venereal disease, because they have no symptoms.

TALKING ABOUT THE RISKS

When you find out your teen is, or is thinking about becoming, sexually active it is time to talk. It is time to assign him some research. An appropriate statement to your teen might be, "I understand that you feel comfortable with your decision to have sex with _____, but I want to be sure you are aware of the risks you are taking, so I am assigning you to do some research. Unless he/she is also a virgin then there is risk of contracting any one of a number of sexually transmitted diseases. I would like you to read up on HIV infection, gonorrhea, chlamydia, herpes, venereal warts, and syphilis. Please write me a report on the symptoms, treatment and possible effects of these diseases if not properly treated". As therapists, we have given such assignments to teenagers. They invariably inform us that they had no idea of all the infections to which they could be exposed. They have also said that they had rethought their decision to be sexually active.

AFTER SEX EDUCATION

If your teenager indicates he is about to become sexually active, take hin to a reputable clinic or agency in your community that specializes in birth conrol, pregancy planning or reproductive services. Ask your family doctor or county health department for the names of such agencies. We recommend you use such an agency to help your teen become aware of the seriousness of the responsibil-

ity he is assuming. Sex is an adult activity and he must be willing and able to handle every aspect of it at an adult level.

Have your teen make an appointment to be seen for education and examination. An exam is particularly important if you think that your teen may already be sexually active.

If your teen is a daughter, we recommend you inquire about birth control shots. The "pill" is too easy to forget to take. Missed pills can be worse than no pills. They may increase fertility. Your daughter also needs to be educated about the use of condoms. While they are not absolute protection, they do provide some measure of protection from HIV and other infection. She has every right to require her partner to use a condom.

If your teen is a son, education about condom use is important for both birth control and disease protection. If your son tries to tell you that birth control is the girl's responsibility, make it clear that he is an equal partner in sexual activity and equally responsible for birth control. He has an obligation to ask his partner if she is using birth control. Every state in the union has child support enforcement laws—and they are getting tougher all the time. Ask your son if a few minutes of pleasure is worth an eighteen year committment to child suppport and fatherhood.

If you sense that your teen's choice to be sexually active is based on pressure from a dating partner, talk about the risks to health and future. Ask your teen if he or she thinks they are both considering the risk to self and each other.

MOTHERHOOD: THE ROAD TO INDEPENDENCE

We talked earlier about teenagers who want to prove their independence. Some teenage girls believe that motherhood will bring them the independence they want. They may actually want to get pregnant. Society inadvertently reinforces this desire by attentive "oohs" and "aahs" given to new mother and child for a short while. If your teenager is adamant about moving out of the house or living by her own rules, she may see having a baby as a means to the independence that she thinks she wants. If you suspect this to be the case you should assign your teen to investigate what support will be available to her and her baby. Make it clear that because you love her and want her to learn to stand on her own feet, you will not provide support for her and a child. She cannot count on you to do so. Rest assured that this is a responsible stand for a parent to take.

Ask to what extent she can depend on the father of the child for assistance with their cost of living. By what means will he get the money? For how long can she count on him to provide for them?

It is dangerous and irresponsible to bring a child into this world without appropriate prenatal care. Medical and hospital bills are costly, even when there are no complications. It is doubtful that any insurance coverage you have for her provides maternity benefits. She needs to research these costs, as well as the average cost of medical expenses for infants and young children. She should present you with a written estimate of these expenses, along with her plan to provide for them.

She should call the state welfare agency in your community and find out about Aid To Families With Dependent Children, commonly known as AFDC. Once she finds out what financial support is available, have her research how much it will cost for her to live on her own by writing out a monthly budget. She can check a local newspaper for the cost of an apartment, car payments, etc. Be sure she includes utilities (and deposits), telephone, food, diapers, baby clothes, car insurance, gas and other expenses she may have to cover. Let your daughter do all of this research on her own if possible. She needs to get the cold hard facts first hand so she will believe them.

If your daughter says she will get a job to support herself, have her check to be sure she can still collect AFDC payments while holding a job. This is also a good time to have her research and apply for jobs for which she is qualified. Help her calculate her monthly income after taxes and social security deductions. Chances are, she will come up in the red.

Getting teenagers to refrain from sex, once they have become sexually active, is diffcult at best. You may also want to assign them writing assignments of your choosing, or some from Chapter 8 of this book. Numbers 6 and 9 on page 78 are certainly appropriate.

What other steps can you take? If you suspect that the parents of the teen with whom your son or daughter is having sex is unaware of the sexual activity, it is probably a good idea to inform them. Express your concerns and your intended strategies. They need to take the same steps that you are taking, in order to also educate their teenager.

If you feel that your teenager is continuing to take excessive risks through sexual activity, and particularly if there are multiple partners involved, it is time to seek professional help.

DRUG AND ALCOHOL USE

All kids today have the opportunity to rather easily acquire drugs and alcohol. When we have polled kids for whom we provide therapy, they gave us estimates on how long it would take to acquire drugs. Almost all could get them at school. The estimated time to buy or acquire ran from five minutes up to no more than an hour. Some said they had only to walk across their own classroom.

The earlier you begin to educate your youngster about the risks of substance abuse, whether it be alcohol or drugs, the better the chance he will choose to resist the temptation.

If you suspect your teen or pre-teen is using, ask them straight out. If the answer you get is "no", then ask him to take a drug test. "If you are clean, I'm sure you would have no problem with taking a drug screening" is an appropriate response. If your teen responds affirmatively, the chances are greater that he is clean, but do the test anyway. If he refuses to cooperate, it is a strong indicator that he may be dirty. You should let him know that this will be your assumption, if he refuses to do a urinalysis. A very frequent and loud complaint is, "You don't trust me." You respond quite honestly, "Because we love you, we simply can't take chances."

Check the yellow pages of your phone book, or ask your doctor for a drug screening lab where you can take your teen for a test. You may want to check with your health insurance provider. Some HMO's and health policies provide coverage at nominal costs. If your teen takes the test but tells you the test might come out positive because of something he ate, drank or medication he took, do not buy it. We remember a young lady who tried to convince us that the test came back positive because she had eaten poppy seed dressing that day.

When you get the results of the screening, ask the lab to interpret them. If the test is negative or a weak positive, take the steps below.

Let him know that he is undermining his trust with you and taking risks with his health and his future, if he does drugs or alcohol. Assign him to write a report on the risks of using substances. He should research the physical effects, short and longterm, the legal risks and the dangers of addiction. Constructive compositions numbers 6 and 9 on page 78 are also appropriate.

Your teen may still tell you that he is not using, or that he "only tried it once or twice". He may even admit that he uses, but it is occasional use and he "can handle it". If you hear any of these replys, assign your teen to attend AA (Alcoholics Anonymous) or NA (Narcotics Anonymous) meetings. Parents need to attend Al Anon, for the sake of their child and for their own sake. If your can find any good articles on drug and alcohol abuse, particularly those told from the first person, assign your teen to read and report on it in writing.

If your teen is using, he has probably taken measures to cover it up. Is his door closed more frequently? Is he burning incense or using air fresheners in his room? It is time to take his door off the hinges. Explanation: "I can't trust you right now. Using drugs is dangerous and you have also been hiding your using from us. Until you prove you are staying clean and living responsibly, you will not have the privilege of privacy provided by a door".

If the drug screening comes back a strong positive you may want to consider professional help, particularly if you see other signs of drug use such as associating largely with kids who use, significant withdrawal from the family, excessive sleeping, drug paraphernalia, personality change, and falling grades. It is also possible your teen will need to go through detoxification. You will need professional help to deal with this level of substance abuse.

TOBACCO ABUSE

You may be wondering why we chose not to include tobacco with other substance abuse. Drugs and alcohol have appeal for kids because they result in an altered state of consciousness. Tobacco tends to be motivated by oppositional and defiant attitudes, as well as by social pressure. Kids are bombarded with marketing gimicks in addition to the pressure they receive from peers.

The combination of peer pressure, advertising and oppositionality are a powerful influence. In addition, tobacco has been determined to be one the most difficult addictions to overcome. Prevention through education is the best insurance that your teen will not smoke or use other tobacco products.

However, if your teen is already using tobacco products, it will be difficult to convince him to stop. You cannot monitor your child around the clock. You can place reasonable limitations on his use of tobacco by establishing "no tobacco" home and car rules. If you see evidence that your teen violates these rules you can assign research papers on the hazards of tobacco use. You can also suspend driving privileges if he uses tobacco in the car. Limit the funds he receives for purchasing the product. If he uses his lunch money, consider pre-paying his lunches at school.

Beyond the restrictions we have mentioned, it will be self-defeating to over-focus on this issue. Ultimately, your teen must decide for himself to give up tobacco.

SUICIDE

So many times we have heard parents say, "I'm afraid he'll go over the edge". When asked what "over the edge" means to them, they often admit to their ultimate fear. Their teen might commit suicide.

Adolescents are especially vulnerable for several reasons:

1. They tend to hold firmly to unrealistic beliefs. These may be realistically dangerous. Included in these are "AIDS and pregnancy can't happen to me", and somehow, "Death doesn't really mean dead."

2. Manipulativeness and impulsivity add to the danger of unintentional self-destruction.

3. Self-absorption and self-centeredness are a very real part of the adolescent developmental stage. "I, my social group, class, school, etc. are the true center of the universe. All else revolves around us."

4. "There is one absolute reason for my being, and as soon as I find it, the world must cave in to its attainment."

5. Low frustration tolerance and the search for a quick-fix, or "I can't stand it."

6. Fear, or "I can't cope."

7. Anger resulting from hurt, fear, or frustration. "And then

they'll be sorry, feel guilty, etc."

8. Desensitization to death; music, cults, TV, or movies that focus on and even glamorize death.

9. The tendency to think in black-or-white, rigid, and absolutist terms, without considering that there are options and many "shades of gray."

10. High drama and over-reactive tendencies.

11. Serious depression, sometimes masked.

12. Drug use; alcohol and many other drugs of choice are actually depressants.

13. Loneliness: the need to belong and to be accepted are especially great during adolescent years.

14. Copy-cat tendencies, when a classmate or teen idol commits suicide.

Despite these and other very valid reasons for concern, we have a word to the wise: Parental over-reaction, over-focus, and hysteria are extremely dangerous, and can even suggest the idea of suicide. Don't!

Sensible, calm parental behavior is indicated. At the same time, you cannot afford to avoid confronting your teen in a supportive and loving manner, if you have legitimate concerns. Significant depression over a period of time, excessive sleeping, or sleep disturbances, important life changes or severe disappointments such as divorce of parents, moving, or failure to achieve a major goal for which the child has worked may be causes of concern.

Reread Chapter 4, which deals with communication, if you like. When the timing seems best, simply say something like, "I've noticed that you seem rather unhappy lately. Would it help to talk to someone about it?" It's usually best to simply accept the teen's response for the time being, even if he refuses help. Be watchful, and hope that he changes his mind. He may. It might be well to have professional resources in mind. For depression, a psychiatrist who is experienced in dealing with adolescents is ideal. Medication or hospitalization may be in order. If your concerns continue, you may decide to become insistent about a professional evaluation.

There are two questions that often mark serious intent: Is he giving prized possessions to others? Does he have a plan, and a means of implementing that plan? An affirmative answer to either of these questions probably indicates the need for a suicide watch. The child should not be left alone, and needs immediate professional help. Inpatient hospitalization may be indicated.

We take all suicide threats quite seriously, and recommend that you do the same.

Manipulative suicide threats are a kind of blackmail. "If you insist on this stupid rule, I will just run away, get pregnant or even kill myself." To win the power game, she stresses her point by scratching her wrist and gulping down forty aspirin.

We usually recommend an immediate trip to the hospital emergency room. A stomach pump is certainly a negative consequence, and much less a lingering problem than stomach or kidney damage from consumption of too many aspirin.

The emergency room choice stresses the very real danger of suicide games. How many pills are too many? How long is too long to wait before she notifies someone of her action? No one knows, and mistakes are quite final.

In the event she is released from the emergency room, rather than admitted to the hospital, a "suicide watch" is in order. She should be accompanied by a responsible adult where ever she goes. Her bedroom door should either be removed by pulling the hinges, or left open at all times. Explain that you love her very much, and she is placing herself in real danger. She has demonstrated that she cannot be trusted at this time to treat herself with respect, and these precautions will continue until she has proven herself to be more responsible. As always, parental self-control and a rational, loving response level is indicated.

SECTION III

CHAPTER 10

◆

POWER BATTLES

It is worth noting that many child and adolescent behavior experts today will tell you to avoid power struggles with your child or teen. If this belief is one you have heard espoused recently, we suggest you think about it.

We all need power and control in our lives. The issue here is knowing the difference between appropriate and inappropriate power and control. Parents must maintain authority, which is very different from an ego or power trip.

WHEN IS YOUR CHILD EXERCISING APPROPRIATE POWER?

A child of five is exercising appropriate power and control when he wants to decide what color socks to put on in the morning or whether to have wheat toast or raisen toast for breakfast. He has enough experience and self control to make these decisions.

A adolescent of fifteen who wants to decide where he is going to live is exercising inappropriate power. He has neither the experience or self control to make those decisions wisely. Likewise, a teenager, who thinks he ought to decide if he should go to school, is exercising inappropriate power. He is demonstrating that he has not yet learned to exercise adequate self-control. Yes, there are times when you need to maintain authority, at least until your teen is responsible enough to defer immediate gratification in favor of long range goals.

Everyone needs to learn to follow the direction or instructions of a higher authority. If your child is not able to work under someone else's leadership, nor mature enough to be a leader himself, then he is going to have difficulty making it in life.

Parents are responsible for maintaining authoritative power. Parents who constantly give in, so they can at all costs avoid a power struggle, are failing to provide their child with the reasonable discipline to which he is entitled. For the moment your youngster may act as though he does not like you. Parenting cannot be a popularity contest and still work in the best interest of the child.

When an individual exercises limited self-control, he often attempts to inappropriately control the people and events in his life. When he has not learned to tolerate frustration or to delay desire for immediate gratification, it becomes difficult for him to have self-control.

"I NEED IT RIGHT NOW"

Frequently, youngsters confuse their wants with their needs. You'll know that your child is struggling with this conflict, when you hear him make statements such as, "I need a new video game". He has confused his wants with his needs.

He believes that his wants must be met immediately, he has not learned that he can tolerate a delay in gratification.

A teen with whom we have worked argues frequently with her mother over many issues. One of her favorite battlefields is food. She never wants to eat what is available at home, claiming argumentatively that she has to (needs to) stop on the way to therapy, school, practice, etc., and get something at her favorite fast food joint. This young lady presents it as a life or death situation because she has confused want with need. Furthermore, she has not yet learned to control her desire for instant gratification.

SORTING OUT THE CONFUSION

The first step to take when encountering this confusion of wants and needs is to remind your teen that he does not need a new CD for his CD player; he just wants one. He does not need a pair of the currently popular brand of sneakers; he simply wants them. He needs to study, do well in school, eat three squares a day, have a roof over his head, have adequate clothing and medical care, and receive reasonable, consistent discipline from you, his parent. If he still insists he needs the item in question, it is a good time for a writing assignment, such as Sensible Sentence number twelve on page 75.

Your teen may try and tell you that his "life will end", or "he can't stand it" if he does not get his wants filled "right now". He is demonstrating lack of toleration for delayed gratification. Sure, there is benefit in instant gratification. Ask any bank who issues a consumer credit card or store who provides revolving credit. They rely on folks who cannot stand to delay gratification. You will be doing your child an important service by refusing to fill his wants immediately. Help him to work toward earning his heart's desire as a more distant goal.

It might be fun and helpful to sit down and watch a little television with your youngster. Point out the way consumer advertising attempts to brain wash us telling us we need what they are promoting.

Offer Choices to Deal with Power Struggles

Your teen may continue to argue his case, but if he does he will do so with greater self-awareness. At this point, it is best to simply offer him a choice between accepting "no" for an answer or earning the money to buy what he wants. This is a reasonable alternative if the item he wants is something he can responsibly possess. If that is not the case, try this: "You may accept my answer of 'no' or you may write me a two page paper on the importance of learning to tolerate delayed gratification". If your child continues to argue inform him you will not listen to any more arguments. Inform him you want his paper by a specified time and walk away.

Getting his wants met is not the only reason that prompts teens and even younger children to argue. Some kids enjoy the rush they get when they can "push an adult's buttons". They like the feeling of power and control that comes with getting others to "lose it" When the adult loses self-control, he gives his power to the kid.

How To Deal With Passive Resistance

Passive resistant behavior is a special category of behavior problem which some youngsters adopt as their preferred style of dealing with conflict. What is passive resistance? It means using inaction to send a message of protest or resistance. The inaction becomes an obstacle to progress.

HOW WILL I KNOW PASSIVE RESISTANCE WHEN I SEE IT?

When you try to discuss your teen's problems with him, and he will only respond with "I dunno" or "I forgot", he is not really telling you that he is ignorant or forgetful. The real message, the one he is not willing to say out loud, is "I don't want to", "I'm not going to", "I'm angry at you", "I want the power and control here", or "I choose to shut the door on communication with you."

CHANGING PASSIVE RESISTANCE

The most effective way of dealing with passive resistant behavior is to ignore the hidden message your child is sending. If the hidden message is still not getting your attention, then your child will have to be open and straight forward if he wants you to understand. Address only the obvious behavior. If your child "forgets" his homework then provide a logical consequence. Give him a reminder bracelet to help him remember.

If he constantly says "I dunno" then assign him "research" (writing assignments) to help him "understand". Most often they find words to express their thoughts orally. At other times it really does help to think more clearly about something "on paper".

THE ULTIMATE ATTENTION GETTING DEVICE

Kids adopt passive resistant styles for many reasons. Some discover its easier than honest communication. Some find its more difficult for their parent to provide consequences to such illogical behavior. But ultimately, kids have found out that it is an effective way of getting their parents attention when nothing else would work.

CHAPTER 11

WHEN YOU ARE AT THE END OF YOUR ROPE

It seems that you have tried everything there is to try. You have tried staying calm, not arguing, giving appropriate consequences, a family agreement, and being consistent. You have tried to stick together as parents. You have reread the chapter on power battles, and paid particular attention to the section on passive resistance. Still nothing seems to be changing, or not enough to relieve the chaos that is going on in your family.

CHANGE YOUR FOCUS

Perhaps it's time to broaden your focus. When our focus is too narrow, it's hard to see what else is going on in our lives. It's easy to ignore the other discomforts in your life, when your youngster's behavior is causing serious problems.

Natural childbirth classes teach women to focus on something outside of themselves, in order to distance from the physical pain within. It is also more comfortable to concentrate on something or on someone outside of ourselves when the pain is emotional. The "problem child's" behavior can serve a valuable purpose. It can function as a center of focus, which permits us to distance from such matters as personal anguish or relationship issues with a spouse.

THE TRIANGLE

Often the kid issue is the primary situation that brings both parents together. They become united in a singular purpose, with both adults focused on the kid. The parents align themselves in such a way as to form a triangular relationship with the child.

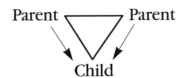

Parents need to work together in order to rear their children, and triads are a frequent form of human interaction. Two people conversing may discuss themselves and express feelings in their one-on-one relationship briefly, but anxiety will develop and increase as their feelings become intense. They can reduce that anxiety by triangulating. One or the other in the diad will typically distance from their intense feelings by bringing up a third person, as the subject of the conversation. Distancing helps us to avoid reacting to intense feelings, and may be temporarily useful in an emotional situation.

Functional triangles are flexible, with the members shifting positions in the triad according to whatever is happening at the time. Rigid or inflexible triangles are stuck, and complicate situations in the long run. A rigid triangle may be used to habitually lower tension between two people in an emotional situation, but it only briefly covers up the true relationship issues between the two.

Triangulation may temporarily lower the anxiety associated with the confrontation of problems, but does not solve the basic problems. Triangles which are motivated by the desire to reduce tension between two of the persons involved, invariably operate at the expense of the third party.

Nevertheless, children need to know that their world is secure. Kids have radar. When they sense conflict in their parent's relationship, they may act out in order to pull their parents together in a united purpose. An illusion of security is created when Mom and Dad unite to "save this child" from himself. The child has become a scapegoat. His self-defeating behavior has been reinforced, and it will probably be repeated.

If you and your spouse are in rigid opposition regarding issues that concern your child, another unhealthy form of the triangle may form. Does the position taken by you or your spouse place one of you in a situation of appearing to "side" with your youngster? If so, your teen may see himself and one of his parents as aligned on two like points of a "triangle" with the other parent on the far end. It becomes easy to fall into a "good guy, bad guy routine", if one parent is seen by the youngster as his ally and the other parent as his enemy.

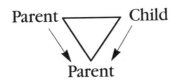

Parent ——— Child

Parent

Conflicts like these usually leave your child believing he does not have to conform to the wishes of the parent with whom he does not agree.

If you are in conflict with your spouse, it may become tempting to keep your child allied with you. It is important to realize that a child becomes a "pawn", if placed in this situation. Not only will you fail to resolve your real issues with your mate, but your child's behavior will probably not change.

TOLERATING YOUR CHILD'S ANGER

Most of us are uncomfortable when others are angry with us. We grow up with the mistaken belief that we are responsible for how others feel. It is important to repeat that the only feelings for which we are responsible are our own.

If your child is angry with you for setting limits or for providing consequences, it is his choice to be angry. He will grow emotionally only when you let him take responsibility for handling his own feelings.

It is easy to allow your discomfort with your child's anger to motivate you to rescue him from his feelings. This is happening when you find yourself compromising or giving in, after you have set limits or consequences. What the youngster learns from this situation is to use his anger to get his way. He learns how to blackmail you, when he realizes that you have difficulty tolerating or confronting his anger.

By learning that you can tolerate your child's anger and discomfort, you will be in a position to help him grow. Help him learn to take responsibility for his own feelings. Give him the clear message that you mean what you say, when you give consequences or set limits.

Both the feeling of anger and the act of confrontation are normal parts of life and of learning. Neither is to be avoided at all costs;

stuffing feelings and avoidance can create more intense problems in the long run. Parenting is a responsibility, not a popularity contest. It is not at all necessary for anyone, even our kids, to be pleased with us at all times.

LIVING VICARIOUSLY

You have seen these parents. They are the ones screaming at their kids during little league games, and urging them on at talent shows and beauty contests. They live their lives through their kids. Perhaps these are extreme and obvious examples, but there are more subtle versions of the same scenario.

Any time you want something for your child more than he wants it for himself, you provide your child an opportunity for excessive attention, feelings of incompetency or oppositionality about his situation. He may feel that his interests, involvement, and efforts are not important. He may cease to care, or to stay involved.

We remember one youngster whose grades and school performance were abysmal. His mother was constantly focused on his school acheivement. She all but did his science project for him, proof read his papers, and corrected his homework (when he got around to doing it). Still, the youngster's grades were terrible. He frequently acted passive resistantly and "forgot" to turn in his work. He made no effort on tests.

This mother was finally able to take an honest and serious look at herself and her own motives. She was experiencing his successes and failures as though they were her own. She saw her teen as an extension of herself, rather than recognizing him as a separate and unique individual.

When she came to understand that she was doing his work for him, this mom backed off. She declared she would no longer take responsibility for Junior's schoolwork. It was time for him to "sink or swim". After some initial floundering, he got it together, and started doing his homework on his own and turning it in. His tests grades came up and he started to show pride in his work. He began to experience academic learning as his own responsibility, and not just a favor he was doing for his mother.

In conclusion, human relations are complex and sometimes it is difficult to "see the forest for the trees". If chaos persists in your family and you still feel "stuck", find a good family therapist with whom you can communicate comfortably and obtain professional help.

CONCLUSION

A POSITIVE PARENTING STRATEGY

Being a parent today does not mean you lose the responsibility or the opportunity to influence your children's social, intellectual, and moral development. Certainly it is true that in two income and single parent families it is harder for parents to spend time with their kids.

No doubt about it, the violence and immorality on TV, the mind numbing effects of video games, and the relentless pressure of kids' peers have influence that did not pose the same problem for Ward and June Cleaver.

We have proposed a *Positive Parenting Strategy* that is practical and effective. It requires only your desire and determination to truly *parent* your child. Raising a child may be hazardous to your sanity, but it may also be well worth the risks. We see it work daily. *It can be done*.

APPENDIX I

STATEMENT OF PERSONAL RIGHTS

Each member of the human family has the right to be treated with respect.

The person and the behavior are not the same thing.

Behaviors may be ineffective, destructive, or unacceptable.

Each person, however, is *accepted* as having worth, dignity, and uniqueness.

Therefore, each person is honorable.

Each individual has the right to be held accountable, and is responsible for his or her emotional state, perceptions and behaviors with their subsequent consequences.

Each person has the right to the feeling of appropriate power, which results from self-control and from owning responsibility for choices, behaviors and their results.

We each have the right to be imperfect, to acknowledge our errors and to grow from them, knowing that our imperfections make us no less respected and accepted as a person.

We grant these rights to ourselves, to every other member of our household and to society.

Signed: _____   _____

_____   _____

Date: _____ Witnessed: _____

THE _____ FAMILY AGREEMENT   **1**
(family name)

Compliance with these basic rules allows me to be a member in good standing of my family and society:

- No physical violence to people or property
- No verbal abuse (cursing, insults or threats)
- No defiance of parents, teachers, or any other authority figures
- No drugs (including alcohol)
- No skipping classes
- No absence from home without permission
- No dishonesty (no lieing, no leaving out important facts)
- No stealing
- No association with acquaintances unacceptable to parents
- _____
- _____

I accept responsibility for abiding by these Basic Rules and understand that any violation of them results in immediate loss of freedom and privileges for a specifed period of time. Parents may assign additional consequences they believe appropriate.

I agree that my freedom and privileges(page 2 of this agreement) shall be determined by the degree to which I fulfill my obligation as outlined in the Weekly Responsibility Schedule attached to this agreement. I also agree that I will attend the Weekly Family Meeting which is held on _____ (day) at _____ (time). I understand that the Family Week begins at the time of this meeting. During the meeting the level of my freedom and privileges for the week shall be determined by totaling the points earned on the previous Weekly Responsibility Schedule. I agree that parents may change the rules specified in this agreement as they deem necessary. Parental decision is final and argument is inappropriate.

Signed: _____ Date: _____
                    (Kid)
Signed: _____ Signed: _____
               (Parent)   *(Parent)*

Entitlements to Minors $\boxed{2}$

We are fortunate to live in a country where most states grant to each person under the age of eighteen years the following entitlements:

1. A safe home in which to reside
2. Three outfits of season appropriate clothing
3. Nourishing food
4. Medical care
5. A continuing education
6. Reasonable discipline

Rights, Privileges, and Responsibilities

♦ Children:

I shall not take these entitlements for granted, because I realize that only a small percentage of the world's population is equally fortunate. Further, I have dignity, respect, and parental love.

Excess (more than three outfits) or name brand clothing, a private room, use of a telephone, transportation, a T.V., spending money, a stereo, entertainment, trips, etc. are not to be confused with Rights or Entitlements. These are Privileges.

Freedom and other Privileges must be earned in our society through wise choices, appropriate behavior, and consideration for others.

If I am to share in the resources of my home and country, I must accept my share of the responsibilities. It is only through assuming responsibilities and by investing oneself that anyone can ever feel a true sense of belonging.

I have read the above carefully, and I understand the differences between Rights, Entitlements, and Privileges.

Signed: _____ Date _____
                    (Kid)

♦ Parental Responsibilities:

I/We agree to provide shelter, food, clothing, medical care, opportunity for an education, and reasonable discipline to our child. We love our child enough to say "NO", and to be directed by concern for his or her long range best interest, rather than immediate gratification.

I/We further agree to withold freedom and privileges, until our child has demonstrated readiness for them by wise choices, acceptable behavior, and consideration for others.

I/We want our child to develop self-esteem, and realize that strict compliance with this agreement is important to his or her feelings of self-confidence and self-worth.

I/We agree to attend and conduct the Weekly Family Meeting to be held on _____ (day) at _____ (time). At this time all points on the previous Weekly Responsibility Schedule will be totaled and rank will be adjusted accordingly. In addition, all changes in the Family Agreement and other family business will be announced and discussed.

Signed: _____ Date: _____

(Parent)

Name:_____   Rank_____   **4**

Date_____ to _____

Responsibilities

PERSONAL	Points	M	T	W	Th	F	S	Su
TOTAL								

Possible Points =   **Total for week____**

HOME and FAMILY	Points	M	T	W	Th	F	S	Su
TOTAL								

Possible Points =   **Total for week____**

SCHOOL or WORK	Points	M	T	W	Th	F	S	Su	**5**
TOTAL									

Possible Points =   **Total for week____**

COMMUNITY	Points	M	T	W	Th	F	S	Su
TOTAL								

Possible Points =   **Total for week____**

GRAND TOTAL = (___) + (___) + (___) + (___) = _____

6

FREEDOMS & PRIVILEGES	RANK 1	RANK 2	RANK 3	RANK 4
Total points per week				

KID ROLE

1. Recognize the difference between entitlements and privileges.
2. Understand that freedom and privileges are earned by responsible and mature behaviors, and not irresponsible behaviors. Our society is based on these concepts.
3. Own responsibility for your attitude, your feelings, your interpretation of a situation, your response to that situation, and for the resulting consequences.
4. Obey the rules and laws in your home, school, and society.
5. Belong to your family. Take appropriate responsibility for jobs that must be done in your home, because you do belong to the family and you share in the family resources.
6. Take good advantage of your opportunity for a continuing education. Learn all you can.
7. Develop your individual identity in a responsible manner. Become good at something.
8. Be reliable. Trust is extremely important.
9. Communicate with your parents and with other family members.
10. Be considerate and respectful to others.
11. Develop self-control, rather than attempting to maintain control over other persons and events.
12. Be the kid. Don't try to parent your parents—your turn will come later.

PARENT ROLE GUIDE

1. Provide or obtain for your children those things to which they are entitled. By law they are entitled to safe shelter, nourishing food, necessary medical care, three changes of season appropriate clothing, a continuing education, and reasonable discipline.
2. Give to your children love, care, supervision, and appropriate physical and verbal affection.
3. Recognize and maintain your position of parental authority. Do so in a mature, rational, and reasonable manner.
4. Model effective problem solving skills and coping behaviors.
5. Establish and maintain rules, limits, and consequences in a consistent manner. Be persistent in enforcing it.
6. Avoid the temptation to give in when your child does not want to hear the word "No".
7. Avoid rescueing children from natural consequences, recognizing that some failure is necessary in order to build frustration tolerence.
8. Avoid doing for others the things that they can do for themselves, in order that they may develop a sense of competence. Assisting them may sometimes be appropriate, however.
9. Recognize that your child is a separate and unique individual , and not an extension of yourself.
10. Deal with your own personal, and/or spousal relationship issues; seek professional help, if necessary. Avoid placing your child in the position of confidante or surrogate spouse. Above all, your child is not a weapon to be used against your spouse in the heat of anger.
11. Do not expect your child to take on age-inappropriate or adult responsibilities.
12. Your child has buddies and friends, they need for you to be their parent. Child-pleasing is a luxury, parenting requires maturity.

BEHAVIOR CHARTS
FOR TOKEN ECONOMIES

Name _____ Date _____

PAY

APPROPRIATE BEHAVIORS	# of _____ sticks, beads, etc.

BREAK

INAPPROPRIATE BEHAVIORS	# of _____ sticks, beads, etc.

PRIVILEGE CHARTS
FOR TOKEN ECONOMIES

Name _____ Date _____

COST

PRIVILEGE LIST	# of _____ sticks, beads, etc

HAVE YOU SEEN THIS PERSON?

CALL 000-0000
If You Know Where He Is

Description:

Note: Please be aware that harboring a minor in your home is against the law!

APPENDIX II

SOLUTIONS FOR SPECIFIC BEHAVIOR PROBLEMS

After reading the previous eleven chapters you should have a basic plan of action for positive, healthy, family growth. You have tools such as the *Family Agreement* to help create a consistent, responsible environment. You have guidelines for dealing with special problems such as fighting and lying. You have improved communications skills.

However, there are still going to be times when you need to address specific behavior problems. These are the times when you will need to do more than just withhold points on the *Family Agreement*, or break a stick. In this appendix are specific behaviors about which parents have frequently requested advice. The format is simple. Below each problem behavior are solutions listed in the order we recommend you try them. Least severe consequences are listed first. Below each solution is a statement you can make to your child, which appropriately acknowledges the behavior and explains the consequences you are giving.

These statements are designed to avoid argument. If your teen attempts to argue with the statement you make when you implement a consequence, then review *Chapter 4, How To Speak The Same Language As Your Child*. Also review *The Role Of A Child* and *The Role Of A Parent* in *Appendix I*, if you like.

Some of the solutions we have offered may seem odd, or even harsh, at first glance. They are all designed to teach kids that their actions have logical consequences. If the behaviors are allowed to persist, society or the self-destructive tendencies themselves will probably deal much more severe consequences. Parenting requires that we look at what may well happen to our kids in the long run.

It helps us to keep a proper perspective when dealing with behavioral issues, if we can see the humor in some of the situations which our kids create. It often helps to include a bit of humor in the consequences as well. Imagine the expression on your teen's face when he comes home and finds his favorite pair of jeans, which he had left laying on the floor, hanging from a branch of the tree in your front yard!

Teens invariably tell us that they much prefer this kind of response in lieu of parental nagging. Besides, if nagging had worked, you would not be reading this. Smile and absolutely refuse to permit anyone to push your buttons. *Do something different!*

AGGRESSION

Your child is aggressive or violent toward others when he is angry or wants his way:

Solution

Aggression may be seen on a continuum from verbal abuse to violence toward objects, self, or others. Refer to the sections on *"The Aggressive Teen"* and *"Too Much To Handle"* in *Chapter 9*.

Aggression and violence indicate a basic attitude of disrespect. If the young person is large or strong and is determined to have inappropriate power and control of the situation, call *911* if you must. Never place yourself or others at risk. Seek professional help.

Statement to your child: *"I love you, but I will not tolerate any violent behavior. You will either calm down and maintain control of yourself, or I will do whatever it takes to help you get yourself under control."*

AWOL

Your child is absent without leave:

Solution

Your teen is not acting in a trustworthy manner if he is absent from home without your permission, or if he tells you that he is one place when he goes somewhere else. Loss of access to his means of transportation is a logical consequence. Remove whatever facilitates his leaving, such as keys and license if he is driving, bicycle if riding one, or shoes if he is walking.

Statement to your child: *"Leaving without asking or letting me know where you will be is irresponsible. Until you can show me that you are acting responsibly, I will keep your _____. Going places will be restricted until I decide differently."*

ATTITUDE

Your child is mouthy, disrespectful and has a poor attitude:

Solution #1

A poor attitude is fundamental to all kinds of behavior problems. Refer to *Chapter 5* on *Family Agreements.* The written statements regarding responsibilities, rights, and privileges relate directly to attitude adjustment, and should be stressed. The structure provided by a written contract is the best way to proceed.

Above all else *"The Statement of Personal Rights"*, which is the philosophical position of this book and of its' authors, should be studied carefully and frequently by all family members. This statement forms the basis for a belief system which spawns constructive attitudes.

Statement to your child: *"Your attitude is unacceptable and self-defeating. We are going to help you adjust your attitude by providing a written family agreement. You will be expected to earn your privileges by acting responsibly and by being a contributing member of the family. When we act more responsibly, we think and feel more positively. A better attitude will result from the changes in your behavior."*

ATTITUDE

Your child is mouthy, disrespectful and has a poor attitude:

Solution #2

Strip your child's room of everything but a bed, chest, desk, chair and alarm clock, and all but three servicable outfits of clothes. Store these things where your teen cannot get to them. Children are only legally entitled to a safe home, medical care, nourishing food, three outfits of clothing, a continuing education, and reasonable discipline.

Statement to your child: *" If you cannot respect the privilege of being part of the family by having a positive attitude, then you will have to manage with only those things to which you are legally entitled. You will be given an opportunity to earn the other things back after you have demonstrated that you no longer take your privileges for granted."*

(If he squeals that he bought something with his own money or that Grandma gave him something else, remind him gently that you are neither charging him for storage, nor for rent on his room.)

BATHROOM

Your child does not clean his bathroom:

Solution #1

Deduct a weekly fee for bathroom usage from his allowance.

Statement to your child: *"If someone else has to do your job then you will be charged for the privilege."*

Solution #2

Set a fee for bathroom cleaning and deduct it from what you plan to spend for your kid each week on special treats, (swimming, movies, pizza, video rentals, etc.).

Statement to your child: *"If you cannot take care of your responsibilities then, I will have to deduct the cost for doing it from what I had put aside to spend on _____this week-end."*

CAR

Your child is reported driving recklessly or gets a ticket:

Solution #1

Take away your child's car keys and driver's license for a month. Allow him to drive only with you or another approved responsible adult in the car.

Statement to your child: *"During the next month you may either find other transportation or drive only when I or another approved adult can accompany you. At the end of that time I expect you to be able to tell me what you think you can do to be a safer driver."*

Solution #2

Remove your child's car keys, driver's license, and driving privilege for at least a month. A driver's license is a "right of passage" in our society. It represents a degree of maturity. Reckless driving is immature.

He can avail himself of public transportation, walk, ride a bicycle, or get a ride with an approved friend (assuming that his friend drives more safely than he does).

Statement to your child: *"For the next month you will have to find other transportation. By the end of that time I expect you to be able to tell me (or write a paper about) what you will do to become a safer driver."*

CAR

Your teen is reported driving recklessly, or gets a ticket:

Solution #3

Buy your teen a bus pass. Many cities have discounted rates for youth passes. If your teen is old enough to drive he is old enough to use public transportation. He will need to obtain a bus schedule. Again, take away driver's license, and car keys.

Statement to your child: *"Until you can indicate what you are going to do to be a safe driver your will have to use other transportation. I will expect you to use the bus pass I have provided you. You can catch a ride with me if I am going your direction but do not expect special ride privileges."*

CAR

Your teen rides with friends who are unsafe drivers:

Solution #1

Buy your teen a bus pass. Many cities have discounted rates for youth passes. Make it clear he may not ride with friends whose driving records are not safe.

Statement to your teen: *"Until you can provide me with a list of friends who have safe driving records, you must not get rides with anyone outside of your family. Please understand that I may decide to confirm the driving records with your friends' parents, because your safety is important to me. If you need to go somewhere we cannot take you, please plan on using the bus. I will provide you with a bus pass".*

CAR

Your child drives without permission, without a license, and/or is under age.

Solutions:

This is dangerous, amounts to auto theft, and is a major liability. Hopefully, there have been no wrecks or injuries. The circumstances under which this occurs vary greatly, but the consequences need to reflect and to teach the seriousness of the situation.

That the teen must work to make restitution for any damages should be obvious. Further, the act is highly irresponsible and indicates little regard for the rights and the safety of others. The rule of thumb is to reduce a person's freedoms and privileges to a level commensurate with his level of immaturity. Once again, the *Family Agreement* may be the technique of choice for the long run. Review *Chapter 5*. Research and writing assignments teach seriousness and develop insight, when used correctly.

Statement to your teen: *This is an irresponsible and selfish act that shows little regard for others. We have decided that your consequences will include loss of the following privileges for_____(length of time):*

_____(privilege)

_____(privilege). You are to cut accident and arrest reports from the news paper on a daily basis for the next month. Each day you will write a one to two page synopsis or summary of the reports for that day. These will be put together as a scrapbook.

CAR

Your child drives without permission, without a license, and/or is under age.

Solution #2

If the act is repeated, it should be reported to the police. It is far better to file charges for a stolen auto against your child, than it is to risk him continuing the behavior and possibly hurting or killing himself or another person. He needs to know in advance that you will do so without hesitation, because you care.

Statement to your teen: *If you cannot take this seriously, we will file charges against you in hopes that the Court can help. We care, and we will be there for you, but we will not rescue you from whatever consequences they give you.*

CHORES

Your child fails to take out the trash when he assigned to do so:

Solution #1
Take all the trash and pile it (in bags) on his bed. Remember, part of your goal is to get his attention!

Statement to your child: *In this situation, no statement is necessary. He should get the message. He knows this is his responsibility. If he complains, ask him the following question: "Do you suppose the trash would be on your bed if you had acted responsibly?" Feel free to ignore the litany of excuses which may follow your question.*

Solution #2
For a kid with wheels, pile the trash in his car. As in solution #1 he should get the message!

CHORES

Your child does not do the dishes when it is his turn:

Solution #1

Pile the dishes in a pan and place them on his bed. He will probably howl about this "injustice" but you will have his attention.

Statement to your child: *No statement is necessary. If he complains or asks, respond with the following question: "Do you think the dishes would be on your bed if you had acted responsibly and taken care of them when you should?" Feel free to ignore the excuses that follow.*

CHORES

Your child does not do the dishes when it is his turn:

Solution #2

Ask your child how much he thinks it is worth to do the dishes each day. After he gives you the amount, inform him you will deduct that amount from his allowance each time he fails to do the dishes.

Statement to your child: *"I will accept your appraisal of the dollar value of this chore. I will deduct that amount from your allowance each time you do not take care of it. Doing the dishes has been assigned to you. It is part of your contribution to your home. If you cannot follow through then expect to pay to have someone else take care of it for you."*

CHORES

Your child does not do his chores or fails to do them in a timely fashion (you can apply this to any or all of his chores):

Solution #1

Set a fee for each chore your child does not handle responsibly. Deduct the fee from his allowance.

Statement to your child: *"If someone else has to do your chores then you will be responsible for paying for it. I will deduct the amount from your allowance."*

Solution #2

Set a fee for each chore your child does not handle. Deduct the fee from what you had planned to spend on treats for your child during the week, a special outing with a friend, a trip to the movies, etc. Be sure your child knows how the money would have been spent had he acted responsibly.

Statement to your child: *"Because you were not behaving responsibly, someone else had to handle your chores. The fee for those chores will be deducted from what I was going to allow you to spend doing_____, this weekend."*

CLOTHES

Your child's clothes or other possessions are left in places they do not belong:

Solution # 1

Pick up the item left laying where it does not belong and lock it up for a week. Return it with the understanding that it will be confiscated for a longer period if it is not kept in the appropriate place.

Statement to your child: *"If you cannot care for your _____, then you will have to do without for a while".*

Solution # 2

Place your child's possessions in strange and unlikely places. If possible choose places that may cause your child some inconvenience (it will help him stop and think next time). A favorite pair of sneakers found in the freezer on a cold winter day can be a real incentive to keep them where they belong.

Statement to your child: *"Yes, that is a dumb place for your _____. But that wouldn't happen if it had been put where it belongs."*

CLOTHES

Your teen is much too focused on his clothes, the brand, style, hairdo, shoes, makeup etc.

Solution #1

Pack away all of his or her clothes and buy three serviceable outfits of clothing from a local thrift shop. Let your child wear these clothes along with a serviceable but least favorite pair of shoes until there is an improvement in attitude and values.

Statement to your child: *"I'm concerned about your values. You seem to be spending so much time focused on the outside of you, that you lack time and energy to develop the important part of you–the part that's on the inside. You will get your clothes, etc. back when I see that your effort and attention to school, home, family and relationships have improved. That includes improved grades, with nothing less than a C on your next progress report".*

CLOTHES

Your child fails to take care of his clothes, fold them, put them away, etc.

Solution #1

Bag up all the clothes your child has left laying around and lock them up for at least two weeks.

Statement to your child: *"You were not taking care of those clothes. I found them_____. I can only assume that you take having nice clothes for granted. I have locked them up until I see from your behavior that you appreciate the clothes you have."*

Solution #2

Put your child in charge of doing his own laundry. Tape simple, easy to follow instructions to the washer and dryer, along with a clear warning, *"CLOTHES MUST NOT BE LEFT IN WASHER OR DRYER"*. Clothing left for an unreasonable length of time may be placed in some imaginative, unreasonable, and outrageous place...enjoy it!

Give your teen one demonstration of how to use the equipment (this eliminates the excuse, "I forgot how"). Make it clear that he will only have clean, presentable clothes to wear, if he takes care of them. Any child who is old enough to read at the fifth grade level can handle this chore.

Statement to your child: *"Because I continue to see that you do not take care of your clothes, I assume that you do not know how. I will show you how to use the washer and dryer and in future you will be responsible for your own clothes."*

CLOTHES

Your child fails to take care of his clothes, fold them, put them away, etc.:

Solution #3

Take away all but three outfits of old but servicable clothing. Require that your child do his own laundry as prescribed in Solution #2.

Statement to your child: *"If you cannot be responsible for your clothes then you will have to do without them. It appears that three outfits of clothing are all that you can handle. You will be responsible for caring for them yourself."*

CLOTHES

Your child wears clothing that is gang related, provocative, or contains inappropriate messages, vulger slogans, promotes drugs tobacco, alcohol, or violence:

Solution #1

Take away the clothing in question and ask your child to write you a paper (age appropriate in length) describing the message he is sending through the clothing in question.

Statement to your child: *"I will keep the _____ you are wearing. The message you are sending by wearing it is offensive/inappropriate. Please write me a _____page paper describing the message you thought you were sending by wearing it."*

Solution #2

Get rid of the inappropriate and tasteless clothing. Keep all money that your youngster has been given to buy clothes. Limit his allowance, if indicated.

Statement to your child: *"I will dispose of the clothing items which you have that are offensive. When you can show me that your judgement has improved, I will let you begin to pick out your own clothes again. Until then, I will keep your clothing allowance and make all clothing purchases."*

CLOTHES

Your child writes or draws on his clothes or other posses- sions:

Solution #1

Remove all clothing or other items except that on which he has written. Explain that when you are sure you can trust him not to write on his possessions then you will return them to him.

Statement to your child: *"When I am sure I can trust you not to write on your possessions or otherwise mistreat them, I will return them to you. Until then you are limited to those which you have already defaced".*

Solution #2

Suspend your child's allowance or money for special treats and privileges until you are certain he is not going to deface his posses- sions.

Statement to your child: *"Until I can be sure you are not going to deface your clothing and other possessions, I am sus- pending your allowance (money for special treats, etc.). I will need the money to replace the things you have destroyed, after you have decided to no longer be destructive".*

DESTRUCTION OF PROPERTY

Your child is destructive at home, writes or carves on furniture and walls, punches holes in his wall or door, etc:

Solution #1

Deduct the cost of repairs from his allowance or money set aside for special treats, new clothes, etc.

Statement to your child: *"I am deducting the cost of the materials for repairing the hole in the wall in your room from your allowance. If you do not want to pay for such repairs then be respectful of our property."*

Solution #2

Buy the necessary materials for repair from your child's allowance and have him do the work of repairing the damage.

Statement to your child: *"It is your responsibility to correct the mess you made by writing on your walls. I have purchased the paint for your room out of your next month's allowance. I expect you to repaint your room."*

DESTRUCTION OF PROPERTY

Your child destroys property as a result of poor anger control:

Solution #1

Have your child make a list of the ways he can handle his anger that are not destructive. Discuss with him when and how he will use these solutions.

Statement to your child: *"Please make a list of other ways you can handle your anger. We will discuss it when you have finished the list. Punching a hole in your door is not acceptable, and it solves nothing."*

Solution #2

Have your child pay for the damage he caused out of his allowance or deduct it from money set aside for special treats, new clothes, etc. Give him the opportunity to make the repair.

Statement to your child: *"I suggest you stop and think the next time you get angry. Punching holes on the wall will not solve your problems."*

"I will take you to the store to buy the materials to repair your wall. The money for the supplies will come out of your allowance. I will show you how to make the repair to the hole in your wall, and you can do the work. Or, I can hire a plasterer to come make the repair and you can pay the bill out of your allowance. Which would you prefer?"

FIGHTING

Your child fights with siblings:

Solution #1

Douse or spray the dueling duo with water. You will get their attention, change their focus, and interrupt the chain of aggressive behavior.

Statement to your child: *"If you can't handle your differences without fighting, then you need to stay away from each other until you can learn to get along."*

Solution #2

Assign each sibling additonal chores to be done immediately.

Statement to your child: *"If you have time to fight, then you must have too much time on your hands. I am assigning you these chores so you can occupy your time constructively."*

FIGHTING

Your child fights with siblings:

Solution #3

Inform both children that they may not be in the same room with each other, until further notice. Set up a simple schedule for use of space in your home. For example, one child eats with the family and the other in his room. They can alternate from meal to meal. When one is watching television, the other must be in his room. If they share a room, then they must take turns sleeping on the couch. After two or three days, call a meeting and discuss with both children whether they have thought of some ways to cooperate with each other. If they cannot make any specific suggestions as to what they can do differently, in order to live together in peace, then continue the separation until they can.

Statement to your child: *"Until you can tell me what you are going to do to cooperate with each other, you must stay in separate rooms. While you are watching TV, your brother will stay in his room. At dinner time one of you can stay in your room and eat, while the other eats with the family. You can alternate on programs and meals. Let me know when you think you have figured out some ways to get along better, and we will discuss them."*

FOOD

Your child will not eat what has been prepared for meals:

Solution #1

Let your child go without eating until the next meal. Do not offer alternatives, and be sure your child does not have enough pocket money to buy junk food once he is out of the house. When he is hungry enough, your kid will eat what is served. You must hold firm, but do not make eating a big issue. Issues mean attention, and attention reinforces the oppositional behavior. Insisting that he eat may turn it into a greater power struggle. Any requests for snacks beyond those normally given should be refused.

Statement to your child: *"You are welcome to wait and eat what is prepared for the next meal, if you do not like this one"*.

Solution #2

Put your child in charge of making meals for the next one to two days, including planning, grocery shopping, and preparation.

Statement to your child: *"If you do not like what is being served, then you can be in charge of planning and preparing meals for the next ____days. Please submit a menu and shopping list for _____'s meals before you go to bed tonight. When do you plan to shop for the groceries you will need?*

FRIENDS

Your teen spends too much time with friends:

Solution #1

Assign your teen to do additional chores. Have a talk about the "time he has on his hands" to spend with friends.

Statement to your child: *"You are spending a lot of time with _____. I think it is important to have time with friends but ___hours a day is too much. If you cannot constructively occupy some of your time here at home, then I must assume you do not have enough to do. Starting immediately you can take over the following chores:____"*

FRIENDS

Your teen spends too much time with friends at the expense of chores, homework, or time with family:

Solution #1

It is time to make it clear to your teen that time with friends is a privilege earned by acting responsibility. Make sure your teen understands that he may not spend time with friends until chores, homework or other obligations and responsibilities are completed.

Statement to your teen: *"Apparently you need some help with time management. In the future you may not spend time with friends here or elsewhere until you have completed your homework and chores. I also expect you to schedule your time with friends so it does not interfere with supper or planned family time. Please check with me and let me know that your homework is complete and chores are done, before asking friends over or leaving to join them elsewhere".*

HOMEWORK

Your child fails to complete or turn in quality homework:

Solution #1

Remove any distractions (TV, radio, stereo, video game, telephone, posters etc.) from your child's room and lock them away until your child's grades improve to a point where all grades are at least a "C", and he is spending adequate time on homework. If he claims he has no homework, have a talk with his teachers or school counselor. Specify a time when you expect your child to be in his room working on homework each week day.

Statement to your child: *"Unless you can find time to complete and turn in quality homework, you are not managing your time adequately . I have helped you by removing some of the distractions from your room until your grades improve. I expect you to be in your room from_____to_____each week day doing homework or studying. I will check your work each evening to see that it is complete."*

Solution #2

Ask for a weekly grade check from your child's teachers. Most school systems are willing to provide a weekly incidental report indicating current grades and any tests or homework outstanding. It sends a clear message to your child that you are in communication with his school and know where he stands.

Statement to your child: *"Until your grades improve I will ask your teachers for a weekly report on your progress. I expect you to be responsible for your schoolwork."*

HOMEWORK

Your child fails to complete or turn in quality homework:

Solution #3

Suspend all after school time with friends until your child's grades improve.

Statement to your child: *"If you do not have the time to spend on your schoolwork then you could not possibly have time to spend with your friends. When you begin to manage your homework and studying responsibly and your grades have improved, then we can discuss your social life."*

HYGIENE

Your child fails to practice good hygiene:

Solution #1

Let him know he will not go anywhere with you so long as he is unkempt and dirty.

Statement to your child: *"If you don't clean up, take a shower, wash your hair and put on clean clothes, you can forget about going anywhere with me including the _____"* (mall, pizza place, any place valued by your child).

Solution #2

Spray him down with the sweetest, cheapest perfume you can find. Do it right before a time he plans to go out with friends. If he has to stay home or go out smelling like a tea rose, he is more likely to take care of his hygiene without you nagging.

Statement to your child: *"I find your appearance and odor to be offensive. Until you begin practicing good hygiene, I will improve on the situation this way."*

LIES

Your teen lies:

Solution #1

Assign your teen to write a paper intitled "What is beneficial about lying". Explain briefly that you are puzzled by his lying, as it only seems to cause him continued grief. This consequence should be given in addition to loss of other basic privileges, or dropping rank if you are using the Family Agreement system.

Statement to your teen: *I am puzzled and concerned by your choice to lie. It only seems to continue to cause you trouble. Please write me a ___page paper entitled "What is beneficial about lying?" Adjust the length to fit your child's age and academic ability.*

Note: See *Chapter 9, "When is a lie a lie?"*. Long standing chronic lying may require professional help.

LIES

Your teen lies:

Solution #2

Communicate to your teen that he has made it clear by his choice to lie that he cannot be trusted. He should immediately lose any privileges which involve a level of trust. For example, you may require that he check in and out with you every time he arrrives or leaves the house. You should also double check any information that he relays to you with a second reliable person. If your teen claims that you are embarrassing him, remind him that it would not be necessary if he had been honest with you. Frankly, he should be embarrassed at his dishonesty. Let him know that you will continue to take these steps until he can show you he is being honest with you. Refer to the section on lying in Chapter 9.

Statement to your teen: *"Your decision to lie to me says that I cannot trust you right now, so I requiring that you check in and out with me before leaving and when arriving at your destination. I will also be checking out all information I receive from you, with someone whom I trust. I will continue taking these measures until I am sure you can be trusted to tell the truth".*

MONEY

Your child insists he can spend his allowance or the money from a job any way he pleases:

Solution #1

Let your child know that as a responsible adult he will not have that luxury. Open a savings account for him, and accompany him to the bank each month to make a deposit from his allowance or his earnings.

Statement to your child: *"People do not get to spend all they earn just as they please. It is important that you learn to be responsible with money by saving some each month."*

Solution #2

Let your teen pay for his own privileges, trendy clothes, entertainment, special snacks and telephone bills out of his own earnings. If he is driving he should pay for his own gas and car insurance. Your child needs to understand that he is only able to spend his money this way because you pay for his essential needs.

Statement to your child: *"It is important that you learn to value and budget your money. In the future you will have to pay for your own privileges. It is only because we pay for your necessities that you are able to spend your earnings on these luxuries."*

ROOM, CLEANING

Your child will not pick up his room or keep it clean:

Solution # 1

Pick up the items left laying were they should not be, and put them in places that are even more outrageous. A favorite pair of jeans found hanging from the tree in the front yard will get your youngster's attention. Humor is important and effective.

Statement to your child: *"Yes, I agree your _____ doesn't belong on_____but it also doesn't belong_____. If you keep it where it belongs, you won't find it on the _____ again."*

Solution # 2

Put the offending items away. When your youngster inquires about them, restrict yourself to only brief comments, such as the statements below.

Statement to your child: (when he inquires about the "lost" object) *"Your what? Was it where it should have been when you last saw it?"*

Statement to your child: (upon return of the "lost" object) *"I wonder if these might be less likely to get lost, if they were kept where they belong. The next time I find them out of place, I will see to it that they get 'lost' for a longer period of time"*

ROOM, CLEANING

Your child will not pick up his room or keep it clean:

Solution # 3

When your child's room is really messy, and nothing else you
have tried worked, pick up the mess and place in a large plastic
garbage bag(s). Lock the bags up for a week.

Statement to your child: *"If you cannot take care of the things
in your room, then you will have to do without them until you
can appreciate both your possessions and your room".*

ROOM, ISOLATION

Your child stays in his room all of the time and will not come out. He isolates in his room to an unhealthy extent:

Solution #1
Remove the door to his room by pulling the hinges.

Statement to your child: *"We love you, and want you to participate with us in our family life. We understand that privacy is important to you, but you seem to be having difficulty finding a healthy balance. When you show us that you can achieve a reasonable balance between being alone and being actively involved in our family life, we will be happy to replace the door to your room."*

Solution #2
Remove everything from your child's room except a bed, study desk, chair, and lamp.

Statement to your Child: *"You seem to be having trouble remembering to be a part of the family. We will help you by removing all of the things from your room that seem to be a part of the problem, such as your _____ (TV, stereo, video games, telephone, posters etc.). You will have to enjoy those activities along with the rest of the family."*

ROOM, ISOLATION

Your child stays in his room all of the time and will not come out. He isolates in his room to an unhealthy extent:

Solution #3

Buy a keyed lock set and replace the door knob on the door to your child's room with it. Lock his room up. Provide him with a change or two of clothing, a blanket, pillow and alarm clock.

Statement to your Child: *"Please consider your room off-limits, until you can learn to behave like a part of the family, rather than spending all of your time in it. You can sleep in the living room and keep your things in the_____."*

ROOM, PRIVACY

Your teen slams the door to his room:

Solution #1

Slamming doors is you teen's way of saying he does not like the fact he is not getting his way. Assign your teen to write a paper for you describing the message he was sending by slamming the door. Have him include descriptions of other more effective and appropriate ways he can express his frustration or anger to you.

Statement to your child: *"Each action we take sends a message to others. Please write me___pages explaining the message you were sending by slamming the door. In addition, please tell me in the paper how you might express yourself more effectively and appropriately".*

Solution #2

Take the door to his room off the hinges and store it away. Let your teen know what his actions say to you, and that the door will not be returned until it is apparent to you that he is   exercising better self-control.

Statement to your teen: *"I am removing the door to your room, because your actions say you do not have the necessary self-control to shut a door without slamming it. When you can behave otherwise to my satisfaction your door will be returned."*

RUNNING AWAY

Your child runs away :

If your child runs away there are several steps you may need to take. We suggest you go back to *Chapter 9, Special Problems*, and read the section, *"I Can Make It On My Own"*.

SELF-DESTRUCTION

Your child is self-destructive, pierces more than his ears, creates scars on his body or is in any other way harmful to himself:

It is time to seek professional help. There are some serious messages being sent when your child takes self-destructive actions.

SEX

Your teen becomes sexually active:

We suggest you go back to *Chapter 9, Special Problems*, and review the section, *Teens and Sex*. Becoming sexually active is a serious issue that requires a considerable amount of attention. It cannot be remedied through one solution.

SMOKING

You find out your child is smoking:

Solution #1

Assign him a paper to write on the health and financial hazards of smoking. Provide him with articles from current magazines and journals to read. Those written by people who have experienced first hand the medical problems that are associated with smoking are the best. Make it clear that you will not allow smoking in your home. Auto insurance rates are also higher for smokers, so inform him he will not be allowed to drive the car until he has stopped smoking.

Statement to your child: *"It has become evident that you are smoking cigarettes. Smoking is unhealthy and risky. I am assigning you to read these articles and write me a report on the health and financial risks associated with smoking. You may not smoke in the house and there will be consequences if you do. In addition, you may not drive the car so long as you continue to smoke. We have a non-smoker's insurance policy, and smoking would raise our rates."*

SMOKING

You find out your child is smoking:

Solution #2

If you think that your child is using his allowance or job money for cigarettes, deduct the amount he appears to be spending on cigarettes from his allowance. Help him open a savings account and deposit his paycheck with only a small amount withheld for spending.

Statement to your child: *"If you are going to waste money on cigarettes then I will deduct the amount you are spending from your allowance. I will continue to do this until I am convinced that you have quit smoking. Or....... Please give me your paycheck to deposit into a savings account. You may have a small allowance from it to spend but not on cigarettes."*

STEALING

Your teen steals from family or others:

Solution #1

Require your teen to write an apology to the person from whom he stole. He should return what he took, or replace it and pay for it out of his own money.

Statement to your teen: *"Stealing is unacceptable. Please write a full apology to _____ and show it to me before you give it to her/him. (The apology should express not only regret but some understanding of the inconvenience or misery caused) In addition, I will expect you to return what you took in the same condition in which you took it. If you cannot do so, you must pay for a replacement out of your own money."*

Solution #2

If your teen has no money of his own then require him to earn the money by working for you at an hourly rate you set. Do not over pay. Require that he do quality work.

Statement to your teen: *"I will expect you to earn the money to replace what you took from _____. You may do the following extra chores at the rate of _____ an hour, until you have earned the money needed."*

STEALING

Your teen steals from a store:

Solution #1

Volunteer his services to work off the value of what he took. Note: If the store is pressing charges and involving the police, it may be time to seek professional help. Simply rescueing him from the consequences is not the best answer, and will probably prolong the problem of stealing.

Statement to your teen: *"We are going to return to the store. There you will apologize to the manager and volunteer to work off the value of what you stole."*

STEREO

Your child plays his stereo (or other electronic equipment) excessively or too loudly:

Solution #1

Remove the equipment from your child's possession and lock it away for a minimum of a week. The possession can be returned when he demonstrates that he can use the item in question responsibly. If the problem is one of playing the stereo too loudly, your child will probably try to argue about what is too loud. That decision is yours and yours alone!

Statement to your child: " *If you cannot use the _____ responsibly (or without disturbing others) then we will have to assist you in learning how. The _____ will be returned when you have had time to think about it and can describe how you will be responsible in using it"*.

Solution #2

See solution #4 for excessive TV watching. The same principles apply here.

Statement to your child: *"If you cannot use _____ responsibly then I will have to assist you in learning how. The plug will be reattached only when you have had time to think about and describe how you will demonstrate using this equipment responsibly in the future."*

SWEARING

Your child swears or uses vulgar language:

Solution #1

Much of the language used by kids today is learned from TV and movies. Limit your child's TV and movie viewing to that which uses clean language.

Statement to your child: *"The language you are using is vulgar and offensive. If this is the language you have learned from watching television and movies, then I will screen what you watch, until you can learn the self-control needed to avoid copying what you hear".*

Solution #2

Have your child write a paper explaining the meaning of each offensive word. Have him list other words that are more acceptable to use in their place. This is a good exercise in thinking and vocabulary development. Many times vulgar expressions are used not just because they sound trendy, but because a youngster is limited in his ability to express himself.

Statement to your child: *"Please write me a minimum of four lines each defining the words _____, _____, and _____. They are vulgar and tasteless, and I doubt that you know their full meaning, even though you just used them. After each word, please list at least two other words that you could use instead. These words should be acceptable in polite conversation".*

SWEARING

Your child swears or uses vulgar language:

Solution #3

Keep a portable tape recorder handy and tape record your child's conversations. Call a meeting and play them back for him. Have him transcribe the conversation onto paper and explain his use of swear words and other vulgar expressions. He can also provide alternative ways of expressing himself.

Statement to your child: *"Your foul language is vulgar and offensive. Please take this tape recording of our conversation and transcribe it to paper. Explain what you meant each time you used foul language, and provide a list of acceptable, polite words you can use in the future."*

TANTRUMS

Your child throws temper tantrums:

Solution #1

Temper tantrums are for pre-kindergarten aged children who have not yet developed any skills for expressing their feelings. If your child is still throwing temper tantrums, then treat him the way you would a five year old. Ask him if he needs for you to lay out his clothes or cut his food. Serve his food at meals on unbreakable dishes and give him a bib to wear. Tuck him in at night and read him a bedtime story.

Statement to your child: *"If you are going to act like a five year old and throw temper tantrums, then expect to be treated like a five year old."*

Solution #2

If you have tried the first solution and are not getting results, then it is time to interrupt the temper tantrum while in progress. Failure to complete the inappropiate chain of behaviors helps the habit deteriorate. Use Grandma's favorite tactic, and toss a glass of cold water on your child. Then hand him the mop and have him clean it up. If he refuse, deduct the cost of cleaning up after him from his allowance.

Statement to your child: *"If you do not like being wet, then learn to express yourself appropriately."*

TELEPHONE, EXCESSIVE USE

The telephone is beginning to grow out of your child's ear:

Solution # 1

If there is a telephone in your child's room let him know that all conversations will be limited to ten minutes, five calls a day (both incoming and outgoing). If he violates the rule then you will remove the telephone from his room. Ask him to log all of his calls with you, including the time the call began and ended and turn the log in to you daily. If you do not receive his cooperation then move to solution #2.

Statement to your child: *"You are not handling your telephone privileges responsibly. Until you can demonstrate responsible use of the phone you will be limited to five calls a day, of no more than ten minutes each. Please keep a log of the times and turn it in to me daily."*

Solution # 2

Remove the telephone from your child's room and lock it up. Suggest more constructive activities to occupy the time freed up by the removal of the telephone. Let him know that all telephone calls will be made only with permission, and only when homework and chores are complete. Let his callers know that he is unable to come to the phone at the moment and will return the call when he is able.

Statement to your child: *"You are not demonstrating responsible use of the telephone. Until you can begin to use more of your time in constructive interests, I will make decisions for you about telephone use. You must ask permission to use the phone until further notice."*

TELEPHONE, EXCESSIVE USE

The telephone is beginning to grow out of your child's ear:

Solution # 3

If your child stays on the phone excessively and fails to get off when asked, simply unplug the phone. You will probably want to cover your ears to protect them from the howls of protest. When your kid calms down, you can make an appropriate statement.

Statement to your child: *"When you can learn to limit your calls to a reasonable length of time, you will not have to worry about them ending so abruptly as this one did."*

Solution # 4

If your child continues to abuse the phone by sneaking off and using other phones in the house, unplug all but the one nearest you. If the problem occurs when your child is at home while you are working, then you may want to consider keeping the phone with you in the car during the day. You can instruct your child to go to a neighbor's in an emergency. Be sure and clue in your neighbors and ask them not to allow your child to make any calls except emergency calls.

Statement to your child: *"Your irresponsible use of the telephone leads me to believe that you cannot be trusted to use it without supervision. Until further notice the phone will not be available to you. It is time to do something more constructive with your time."*

Note: We do not recommend removing all phones if your child does not have other ways of communicating with an adult in case of an emergency.

TELEPHONE, UNAUTHORIZED CALLS

Your child runs up long distance telephone bills:

Solution #1

Inform your child that his telephone privileges are suspended until the bill he ran up is paid. Deduct the bill from his allowance or suspend his allowance until the bill is paid.

Statement to your child: *"You have shown us that you cannot use the telephone responsibly, so we will have to suspend your telephone privileges until we think you have learned to handle it appropriately. In the mean time the bill you ran up will be deducted from your allowance."*

Solution #2

Inform your child that his telephone privileges are suspended until he works off the bill he ran up. Allow him to do extra chores for which he would not normally be responsible (don't let him out of his regular chores!) and pay him a reasonable wage.

Statement to your child: *"You have shown us that you cannot use the telephone responsibly, so we will have to suspend your telephone privileges until we think you have learned to handle it appropriately. We will credit your allowance towards the bill and you can work off the rest at a reasonable wage doing extra chores."*

TELEPHONE, UNAUTHORIZED CALLS

Your child runs up long distance telephone bills:

Solution #3

Inform your child that his telephone privileges are suspended until he can find a way to earn money to pay for the bill. Insist that he also pay a deposit in advance equal to at least half of his last bill. Your child will probably protest this to be unfair, but it is just exactly what the telephone company expects of their adult subscribers.

Statement to your child: *"Because you ran up telephone bills irresponsibly, your telephone privileges are suspended until you can find a way to earn money to pay off the bill you owe, and to make a deposit towards any future bills."*

TELEPHONE, 900 NUMBERS

Your child runs up bills on 900 sex lines or other 900 lines:

Solution #1

Inform your child of the charges you have received on the phone bill. Let him know that you will be taking all phones with you when you leave the house, and at night. Instruct him to go to the neighbor' house if he has an emergency and needs to call you.

Make it clear that he will not have telephone privileges at home until he can prove that he can be trusted with the phone. Give him opportunities to demonstrate responsible use of the phone in your presence. Have him write a paper for you on the topic, "What Is Wrong With Calling 900 Numbers?".

Statement to your child: *Because you have run up charges for this 900 number on the telephone bill, I will be taking the phones with me whenever I leave the house. When you can demonstrate responsible use of the phone in my presence I will consider allowing you telephone privileges. In addition, I expect you to write a paper, ___ pages in length entitled 'What Is Wrong With Calling 900 Numbers?'.*

Note: We do not recommend removing all phones if your child does not have other ways of communicating with an adult in case of an emergency.

TELEPHONE, 900 NUMBERS

Your child runs up bills on 900 sex lines or other 900 lines:

Solution #2

Inform your child of the charges you have received on the phone bill. Make it clear that he has violated your trust and acted irresponsibly in his use of the phone. Let him know that all charges will be deducted from the money budgeted for his car insurance until the bill is paid. Suspend his driving privileges and use the insurance money to pay for his phone charges.

Statement to your child: *"The 900 charges you have incurred on the phone bill are irresponsible and a violation of my trust in you. I will use the money budgeted for your car insurance to pay off your phone charges. For now, your driving privileges are suspended. Please give me your car keys and driver's license".*

TELEPHONE, 900 NUMBERS

Your child runs up bills on 900 sex lines or other 900 lines:

Solution #3

Remove all telephones from your home and take them with you when you leave the house. Sit down with your child and explain he will have to pay for the charges he ran up. Ask him to provide a plan detailing how and when he will pay you back. The plan should include at least a 50% deduction in his allowance. If he protests that he did not make the calls, ignore it. If he cannot come up with a plan, then begin deducting the charges from his allowance and/or budgeted expenditures for his clothing and extracurricular activities.

Statement to your child: *"Our telephone bill indicates that you have run up $_____ in calls to a 900 number. I would like to know how you plan to pay for these calls. I expect you to provide me with a plan by tomorrow at the latest detailing how and when you will pay me back. I expect, as part of the plan, that you will include forfeiture of at least half of your allowance starting immediately. If you cannot come up with a plan then I will begin deducting the amount from your allowance and from the money I give you for weekend activities with friends."*

Note: We do not recommend removing all phones if your child does not have other ways of communicating with an adult in case of an emergency.

TELEVISION

Your child watches TV excessively or ignores your direction to turn off the set and do his chores, etc.:

Solution # 1

Walk over and turn the TV OFF! Your child will probably protest but ignore it. If he tries to turn the TV back on then it is time to move to the next solution.

Statement to your child: *The TV is on excessively, so I will have to help you manage your TV time until you can act more responsibly. I will let you know when you can watch TV again."*

" Now let's take a look at your homework. Is it complete? Are there assignments on which you can work ahead? If your home-work is complete let's find a book for you to read, a game to play, or you can go outside and get some exercise."

Solution # 2

Remove the TV from the room and lock it up for a week. Expect your child to find more constructive activities. Return the TV with the understanding that he must use his time responsibly and watch TV selectively.

Statement to your child: *"I am removing the TV for the next week. For the next seven days I expect you to demonstrate that you can use your time for more constructive interests. You can read, exercise, do homework, find a hobby or craft. I'm open to ideas. I expect you to demonstrate that you are not going to abuse TV watching privileges when the TV is returned".*

TELEVISION

Your child watches TV excessively or ignores your direction to turn off the set and do his chores, etc.:

Solution #3

Remove the TV from the room and lock it up. Let your child know that the TV will be returned only when he demonstrates constructive use of his time.

Statement to your child: "I am removing the TV until you can demonstrate that you can use your time more responsibly. You can read, do homework, exercise or find a hobby. When you can demonstrate responsible use of your time then TV watching privileges will be returned."

TELEVISION

Your child watches TV excessively, has not responded to solutions 1, 2 & 3:

Solution #4

Unplug the TV first. Hold the cord up high where your child can see, and then cut the plug off with a large pair of scissors. Use a dramatic sweeping motion!

At this point you should have your child's attention so you can explain that TV watching is suspended until he can learn not to abuse his TV watching privileges. You can very easily attach a new plug when you choose with an inexpensive device you can purchase at a local discount or hardware store. If you have more than one TV in the house, you may want to follow this procedure for all of them.

Statement to your child: *"If you cannot manage your TV time responsibly then I will assist you until you can demonstrate that you can. You need to find more constructive ways to use your time such as homework, baby-sitting or mowing lawns for spending money, reading, or a constructive hobby."*

TIME, LATE FOR BEDTIME

Your child does not get to bed on time:

Solution #1

Remove any activity that is distracting your child at bedtime. See solutions for excessive TV watching, telephone use, etc.

Statement to your child: *"Because you continue to let _____interfere with getting to bed on time, we will assist you in making more responsible choices."*

Solution #2

If your child is simply wasting time getting to bed as a result of stalling tactics, subtract the time from privileges.

Statement to your child: *"If you cannot get to bed in a reasonable length of time, then I will have to subtract the time you waste from your _____(telephone, TV, game, play, etc.)time." This solution is particularly useful if you are using the Family Agreement.*

TIME, MISSES CURFEW

Your child breaks curfew, comes in late:

Solution #1

Suspend all free time outside the home for a week. Exceptions, of course, are school and work. By the way, whether your child is late is determined by your watch not by his.

Statement to your child: *"If you cannot be in on time then you will have to stay at home."*

Solution #2

Lock up your child's bicycle, (skateboard, rollerblades) for a week.

Statement to your child: *"Having the privilege of spending your free time unsupervised seems to be too difficult right now. Until you think through how you will handle it better, you can do without your bike and stay at home."*

TIME, MISSES CURFEW

Your child who is on foot breaks curfew, comes in late:

Solution #3

Take away your child's favorite sneakers (they are a big peer status symbol now days!) for at least a week.

Statement to your child: *"You cannot seem to remember to return home on time, so I will help you remember by putting your _____ shoes away for a while."*

Solution #4

Take away your teen's car keys and driver's license for a week.

Statement to your teen: *"If having the privilege of driving the car interferes with being responsible enough to be home on time, then you will have to find other transportation."*

TIME, OVERSLEEPING

Your child does not get up on time:

Solution #1
Being doused or sprayed with cool water usually does the trick.

Statement to your child: When your child protests just say, *"It won't happen again if you get up on time"*.

Solution #2
Several parents have suggested: keep a bag of marbles in the freezer. When your child refuses to get out of bed, lift the covers and dump the marbles in the bed. They have an effective way of rolling right to the center! (We haven't tried it—just find it amusing, so we pass it along.)

Statement to your child: *"It won't happen again, if you get up on time."*

TIME, TARDY

Your child misses the school bus frequently:

Solution #1

Take your child half of the way to school. Have him get out and walk the rest of the way.

Statement to your child: *"You can get out of the car and walk the rest of the way. The next time you miss the bus you will walk the entire way and deal with the consequences of being late."*

Solution #2

Let him walk to school! Yes, he may be late and get detention. A detention will act as an additional reinforcement to be at the bus on time.

Statement to your child: *"You missed the bus? I guess you will have to walk. That is unfortunate. You may get a detention if you are late."*

Note: If your child is missing the bus on purpose, please review Chapter 10, Power Battles, pages 112-113. Your teen may be acting passive resistantly.

TIME, TARDY

Your child is frequently not ready for school on time:

Solution #1
Let your child be late. If he misses the bus, let him walk. Let him deal with the consequences of being tardy at school.

Statement to your child: *"If you cannot be ready for school on time you will have to deal with having a detention at school when you are tardy."*

UNAUTHORIZED PURCHASES

Your child charges merchandise by phone, computer, magazine ads, etc. without your knowledge or permission:

Solution #1

Suspend your child's telephone privileges and allowance until the bill is paid.

Statement to your child: *"It is not responsible to run up bills when you cannot pay them. Until you can learn to use the telephone responsibly your telephone privileges are suspended. The bill you accrued will be deducted from your allowance until it is paid."*

Solution #2

Remove all telephones from your home when you cannot be there. Inform your child that all telephone privileges and other privileges are suspended. Stop your child's allowance and deduct it from the bill. Tell him his privileges will not be reinstated until he finds a part time job and earns the money to pay back what he owes.

Statement to your child: *"If you are going to act irresponsibly then I will have to remove your privileges until you can handle them more maturely. Your bills will be deducted from your allowance. In addition, you need to find a way to earn some money to help pay what you owe. Responsible people do not run up bills they do not have the means to pay."*

Note: We do not recommend removing all phones if your child does not have other ways of communicating with an adult in case of an emergency.

INDEX